Cold Burial

A Journey into the Wilderness

CLIVE POWELL-WILLIAMS

VIKING

VIKING

Published by the Penguin Group
Penguin Books Ltd, 80 Strand, London WC2R 0RL, England
Penguin Putnam Inc., 375 Hudson Street, New York, New York 10014, USA
Penguin Books Australia Ltd, Ringwood, Victoria, Australia
Penguin Books Canada Ltd, 10 Alcorn Avenue, Toronto, Ontario, Canada M4V 3B2
Penguin Books India (P) Ltd, 11 Community Centre,
Panchsheel Park, New Delhi – 110 017, India
Penguin Books (NZ) Ltd, Cnr Rosedale and Airborne Roads,
Albany, Auckland, New Zealand
Penguin Books (South Africa) (Pty) Ltd, 5 Watkins Street,
Denver Ext 4, Johannesburg 2094, South Africa

Penguin Books Ltd, Registered Offices: 80 Strand, London WC2R 0RL

First published 2001
1

Set in 13/15.5pt Monotype Fournier
Typeset by Rowland Phototypesetting Ltd, Bury St Edmunds, Suffolk
Printed in Great Britain by Clays Ltd, St Ives plc

A CIP catalogue record for this book is available from the British Library

ISBN 0-670-88564-9

To Ronnie Taylor, Historian, Scotsman and Friend

Contents

List of Illustrations

White-faced musk-oxen in defensive formation (Mowbray Critchell-Bullock).

Jack cleaning wolverine skin in 1924 (Mowbray Critchell-Bullock).

The north end of Artillery Lake, autumn 1924 (Mowbray Critchell-Bullock).

Jack cracking bones for marrow (Mowbray Critchell-Bullock).

Jack, with Whitey, launching a loaded canoe on the Thelon, 1925 (Mowbray Critchell-Bullock).

Artefacts presented by Jack to the National Museum, Ottawa (Mowbray Critchell-Bullock).

Jack portaging under a maximum load (Mowbray Critchell-Bullock).

A page from Edgar's diary (Dover College).

Cabin on the Thelon built by Jack, Harold and Edgar, October–November 1926 (Hazel Lunt).

Graves dug by RCMP patrol, June 1928 (Hazel Lunt).

MAPS

Foreword

It was nine years ago when Ronnie Taylor, the Dover College historian and archivist, first showed me Edgar Christian's diary. I had just completed my history of St Martin's School, Northwood, *With All Thy Might*. Ronnie greatly assisted me in my research at Dover, where the founder headmaster of St Martin's, Lionel Woodroffe, had enjoyed a happy school life.

As I dipped into the diary, I was appalled by the hardships and privations suffered, so understated and couched in an immature schoolboy hand. Later I learned of the diary's miraculous survival in the cabin by the Thelon River.

That document from the remote Canadian wilderness, now resting in an English public school, spurred me to find out more. Gradually the story unfolded of young Edgar Christian, his enigmatic cousin Jack Hornby, and the moody Harold Adlard. My journey took me to Nantwich, Cheshire, Bron Dirion in North Wales, Harrow School, the Canadian National Archives and many other places.

I am indebted to all those people who have aided me on the way, especially the Christian, Adlard and Critchell-Bullock families, who have been most generous with the loan of private papers. Also the headmasters of Harrow School and Dover College, my editor, Kate Jones, at Viking Penguin, my agent, Gill Coleridge, and Robin Blake, for all his help. All others are mentioned in my Acknowledgements.

But none of this would have been possible without Ronnie and his unstinting support, and it is to him that this book is dedicated. Of course, without the patience and understanding of my wife, Kay, and my children, Kate and Andrew, I would not have completed the task.

Clive Powell-Williams, Northwood, 2001

Acknowledgements

CANADA

For their intimate knowledge of the Thelon Game Sanctuary and travel along the Thelon River, thanks to Alex Hall of Canoe Arctic Inc., Professor Stuart Mackinnon of the University of Alberta, and especially David Pelly, who has provided wise counsel over the years. From the Canadian Heritage Rivers Secretariat and Parks Service: Max Finkelstein, Michael Greco, Bob Gamble and Ronald Searle. From the National Archives of Canada, Ottawa: Michael Mac-Donald, James Kidd, Debbie Shaw and Aileen Spitere, and independent researchers Jody Perrun and Susan Villeneuve. Anne Parmenter of Canadian Pacific, for details on the Chateau Laurier, Ottawa and SS *Montrose*. Anne Ross, for material on her father, Harry Wilson. For their general interest, Judith Kennedy, the late Jack Coughlin, Cathy Richardson, Debbie Forrester and Lawrence Jeffery.

AMERICA

For obtaining and compiling copies of the annotated version of *Unflinching*, thanks to Patsy Carter of Dartmouth College, Stefansson Collection and Dr Stewart Hamilton.

Acknowledgements

KENYA

For reports on the death of Captain J. C. Critchell-Bullock, thanks to Roger Hartley, headmaster of Kenton College, Nairobi, Jan Hemsing, archivist of the Norfolk Hotel, Nairobi, and Leah Rotich of the Kenyan High Commission.

UNITED KINGDOM

For the educational background of Edgar Christian, Jack Hornby and Harold Adlard, thanks to the headmasters of Dover College, Martin Wright and Howard Blackett, and their archivists, Ronnie Taylor and Michael Vanderhoeven; the headmasters of Harrow School, Nick Bomford and Barnaby Lenon, housemaster David Elleray, and particularly the school archivist, Rita Gibbs, for all her labours. Also the archivists at Bradfield and Lancing Colleges.

For their painstaking research into the Hornby family, thanks to Peter Wall and W. H. Hoole. Also Gordon Fergusson for information on the Cheshire hunting scene, and the archivists at Blackburn Rovers FC, Surrey CCC and MCC, Lords.

I owe a great debt to Hazel Lunt, the late Perpetua Ingram and other members of the Christian family for the loan of papers, documents and photographs, and for their supportive interest throughout.

Thanks to Wilfred Williams and his late wife Maud, for their friendship and wealth of detail on the Christians' life in North Wales; the late Mona Williams; Canon Idris Thomas of St Beuno's Church; and Mrs Hughes, owner of Bron Dirion, for her hospitality during my visit there.

I am grateful to Tony Adlard, Michael Stamford and other

members of the Adlard family for the supply of documents and photographs on Harold Adlard. Also Jan Keohane, Assistant Curator at the Fleet Air Arm Museum, Yeovilton, for Harold's war records.

Thanks to Mowbray Critchell-Bullock, for his father's diary, expedition typescript, biographical sketch and photographs.

For their advice on Arctic exploration: Dr David Walton, Geoffrey Hattersley-Smith, Bob Headland, archivist of the Scott-Polar Institute, Cambridge, and Patrick Walcot; and George Spenceley, for his canoe trip down the Thelon and for supplying photographs. For his survival expertise, Andy McNab; on malnutrition and its effects, I am most grateful to Dr Martin Sweatman and Dr Mike Stroud.

Finally, thanks to a variety of people for their help in so many ways: Hans Baumann, Richard Gallimore, Jeffrey Bailey, Tony Carne, Tim O'Mara, Roy Fossett, Chris Swinson, Jean Edwards, Iain Robb, Michael Hodgson, Stuart McLean, David Cornwell and especially the late Tony Colwell, John Ford, Michael Dugdale and Marilyn Moorhouse.

Note on the Text

Edgar Christian in his diary followed the convention of the British Empire as a whole by expressing temperature on the Fahrenheit scale. For consistency I have adhered to this convention when quoting all temperatures: 0 degrees Fahrenheit is −17.7 degrees Celsius.

In the mid-1920s, the terms 'Indian' and 'Eskimo' were universally acceptable. I have similarly adopted the usage of the time.

In quotations from Edgar's diary, some of his idiosyncratic spellings and punctuation have been retained.

YUKON
TERRITORY

Great Bear Lake

Coronation Gulf

Coppermine R.

NORTHERN   TERRITORY

Mackenzie R.

Artillery Lake

Thelon R.

Schultz L.

Great Slave Lake

Dubawnt R.

Baker

BRITISH

COLUMBIA

FORT SMITH
4–8 JUNE

Slave R.

FITZGERALD
3 JUNE

FORT CHIPEWYAN
1–2 JUNE

FORT McMURRAY
27–28 MAY

Athabaska R.

WATERWAYS
25 MAY

Lake Athabaska

EDMONTON
11–24 MAY

A L B E R T A

SASKATCHEWAN

MANITOB

CANADIAN

Calgary

WINNIPE
6–9 MA

Vancouver

PACIFIC

U N I T E D   S T A T E S   O F

The Canadian Pacific Railway
showing Harold and Edgar's halts with dates

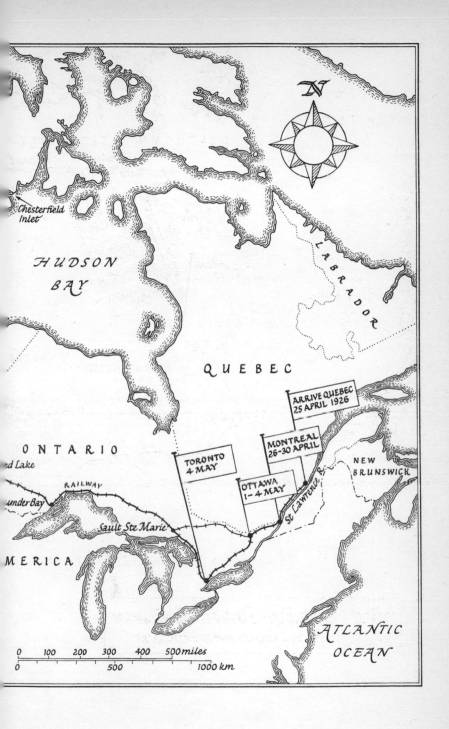

CHESTERFIELD
INLET

HUDSON
BAY

LABRADOR

QUEBEC

ARRIVE QUEBEC
25 APRIL 1926

MONTREAL
26–30 APRIL

ONTARIO

TORONTO
4 MAY

OTTAWA
1–4 MAY

NEW
BRUNSWICK

RAILWAY

ed Lake

under Bay

Sault Ste Marie

St Lawrence R.

MERICA

ATLANTIC
OCEAN

0   100   200   300   400   500 miles
0   500   1000 km

Upon the journey of our life half way
  I found myself within a gloomy wood
  For I had missed the path and gone astray.
How hard to make that forest understood . . .

DANTE ALIGHIERI,
Inferno, Book I, lines 1–4,
translated by the sub-Arctic explorer Warburton Pike

All men dream: but not equally. Those who dream
by night in the dusty recesses of their minds wake in
the day to find that it was vanity; but the dreamers
of the day are dangerous men, for they may act their
dreams with open eyes, to make it possible.

T. E. LAWRENCE

1. Hornby of the North

In the winter of 1924, surrounded by a vast sub-Arctic wilderness, Captain James Critchell-Bullock sat inside the dug-out that he and his travelling partner John Hornby had excavated with their own hands. Wrapped to the best of his ability against the intense cold, he was writing in a folio notebook – his journal. It was Christmas Eve.

The captain, late of the Indian Army's 18th Lancers, was meditating gloomily on his position. The dug-out was collapsing. Food and fuel supplies were low and his dog was dying. He was otherwise alone.

> Alone in a dug-out beneath the sand and snow when but one thousand miles away homes are alight with fairy lights and decorated with those little frills pertinent to Christmastide.

Looking up from the page, he tried to visualize festivity. In a hazy, golden montage, Christmases past rose before his mind – fat dogs panted before huge log fires, aunts gossiped interminably, uncles slumped and snored in armchairs. He heard Christmas carols and hunting horns. He smelled roast goose, a balloon of good brandy, spruce needles in the carpet.

He glanced moodily upwards at the ominously sagging roof of his present dwelling. At any moment it might give way, cascading three tons of icy gravel on top of his head. Shifting to a more comfortable position in this cramped space, he inadvertently tipped one of the crazily misshapen spars that propped the roof. Sand spattered around him on the frozen floor and he stiffened until the sand stopped falling. Then he resumed his meditation on solitude and desolation.

> Alone in this awful shack of continual discomfort with its subsiding walls and crazy roof, likely at any moment to fall and entomb me in a living grave. Alone with sufficient wood to make only one more fire. Alone with a dying dog whose foot is stinking with the decay consequent on frostbite. Alone with but the howl of the blizzard outside to cheer me and the thoughts of peace and happiness and the faces of loved ones coming to mind – only to remind me more and more of my deep loneliness.

The underlying reason for Critchell-Bullock's precipitate descent into misery is not explicit here. Certainly the cold was very bitter – minus 30 degrees Fahrenheit is not unusual in these latitudes. Bad weather could imprison a man inside for days at a time and the cabin was a place of little ease. Dimly lit by 'candles' fashioned from string and fox fat, the interior stank of greasy smoke, suppuration and eviscerated game, while the constant fear of bringing down the roof restricted any freedom of movement. Yet it was neither cramp, nor cold, nor even hunger, that gnawed most at Critchell-Bullock's spirit. It was Hornby.

Jack Hornby was his expedition partner and the senior man. He was supposed to provide inspiration and help, yet he was not here. In fact, the matter was worse even than simple dereliction. Critchell-Bullock had hero-worshipped Hornby, and the expedition had taken all his money. He was being repaid with nothing but bitter disillusionment.

Critchell-Bullock, at twenty-six, was a veteran not only of the Western Front, but of the Palestine campaign and the Desert Mounted Corps. He had retired from the army in the summer of 1923 and had come to North America in the hope of a brighter future, combining suitable adventure with reputation and profit. His encounter with Hornby had occurred in Edmonton just a few weeks after landing, when they had come upon each other in the restaurant of the King Edward Hotel.

This interesting new acquaintance, Critchell-Bullock gathered, was the forty-three-year-old son of a famous cricketer back in England. But many years earlier, Hornby had rejected his wealthy background for the frontier life, specializing in winter travel of a kind not for faint hearts. Accessible only by canoe and dog team, his favourite resort was the Barren Lands, otherwise known as the Barren Ground or, simply, the Barrens: a frozen hell so harsh and ruthless as to cut down any white man or Indian unable to match it in the game of jeopardy and survival. Such terms might have been calculated to attract Critchell-Bullock's interest. He was actively seeking new sporting challenges, more extreme than anything he had encountered before.

He quickly decided that, in Hornby, he had found his

guide and mentor. Hornby had, according to his own often-repeated claim, 'out-Indianed the Indians' in order to make the Barren Lands his own. The claim was even substantiated by articles about him in the Edmonton press. There were other men – trappers, adventurers – who could make a similar case, but none had the public charisma and private charm of Jack Hornby.

Hornby was, by any standards, a man out of the ordinary. Only five foot four, he had developed over many years a down-at-heel, Chaplinesque image. He let his curly hair grow long and tangled. He wore ragged trousers and old tailor-made shirts filched from his father, and sported a grubby overcoat with a moth-eaten astrakhan fur collar, of a cut long out of style. On the rare occasions when he visited London, he would turn up at a smart hotel attired in this way for luncheon appointments and escape being bounced by the porter only by virtue of his faultless old-Harrovian vowels. Hornby's wardrobe became a few degrees less shabby as he got older – since the War he had always travelled with a dinner jacket, even into the Barrens – but the contrast between that impeccable upper-class accent and his dishevelment was nevertheless striking. Socially, he was often withdrawn, but just as frequently there were phases of sparkling humour and vivacity and, at these times, everyone was struck by his piercing blue eyes. Although normally bare-headed (in an era when men universally wore hats), he sometimes adopted a shapeless peaked cap that, in photographs, gives him the anachronistic look of a beatnik. The image is not inappropriate. Hornby was in all essentials a prototype drop-out.

From such material, myths spring up, compounding truth and imaginative embellishment. This was the man who had, on one occasion, run a hundred miles in twenty-four hours and, on another, raced a train on foot for a bet. In 1913, guiding two French missionary fathers who were attempting to make contact with the natives of Coronation Gulf on the Arctic Ocean, he had outfaced an Eskimo who was determined to murder them all.

The Great War gave added impetus to Hornby's fame. After volunteering as a private soldier, he'd shipped to the Western Front, been gassed at Ypres, taken a commission, and won a Military Cross at the Somme. Back in postwar Canada, he had canoed to the uninhabited eastern end of Great Slave Lake, built himself a cabin and survived alone through two of the coldest winters on record. At one point the thermometer dipped to −62°F. At another, weakened by starvation, he crawled on all fours across half a mile of lake ice to lift his fishing hooks.

Within a few days of their first meeting, Critchell-Bullock had convinced himself that he was destined to travel with this living legend, and he at once made a pious resolution. He vowed to:

> devote my time, energy, and money to a series of investigations, and to be satisfied as recompense with the pleasure of having been instrumental in placing on record a survey of the life and activities of a man who knew more about the natural phenomena in the Treeless Northern Plains than any other man living.

Hornby was flattered, of course. Critchell-Bullock was a younger man of his own class who, in the army, had already known some rugged living, but desired to test himself against even greater hardships. He also had money to invest in a suitable expedition. Hornby decided to take him on, and the pair became inseparable around Edmonton.

They hatched a scheme for a two-man scientific and trapping expedition into the Barrens, even securing a modest government commission to report on geophysical conditions, climate and wildlife. In addition they meant to trap furs, which, said Hornby, would earn them a fortune on their return. At the same time, Critchell-Bullock meant to make commercially valuable cinematographs of the rarely seen Barren Ground fauna. So it was in the triple expectation of esteem, adventure and profit that they assembled their outfit – seven tons of equipment at a personal cost to Critchell-Bullock, so the captain claimed, of $40,000. The game was afoot.

It was summer 1924 when the pair canoed north to Fort Reliance, the then-deserted trading post at the end of Great Slave Lake, and from there proceeded up a steep portage to the level of Artillery Lake, which extends northward as far as the Barrens. At its far end, a few miles above the watercourse which connects Artillery and Ptarmigan Lakes and is known as the Casba River, they constructed their ramshackle dug-out and settled in for winter.

The Barrens offered many experiences of extraordinary beauty, even of epiphany. One clear, still winter evening, across two miles of snowscape, they saw through hunting glasses the eyes of a wolf pack glinting in the setting sun.

Alone at night in their sleeping bags, they listened to the whisper of mouse paws running through a maze of tunnels two feet beneath the snow. They gazed at the Aurora Borealis and heard, from a distant river, 'ice cracking like big guns'. In summer heat, they watched the rare and secretive musk-ox roaming its favourite habitat, rattling through the willows on the banks of the Thelon River, bellowing and burbling as it went. And they saw with amazement the mighty seasonal migration of the caribou herds, when, over a couple of days, two thousand animals thundered past the camp in a haze of dust and flies. If a lake or river blocked their path, the caribou plunged unhesitatingly in and swam for it, their tails lifted fastidiously out of the water.

But, for all these marvels, Critchell-Bullock quickly discovered the innumerable ways in which that dismal country could depress and torment him. In summer, there was the heat and savage biting flies, and in autumn torrential rain, smothering snow and ferocious wind, 'as bad as the torque side of a fast plane'. During the eight-month winter they faced the cold with minimal resources of food and fuel, and the quality of their shelter was a chronic worry. This tiny, shifting and unsafe structure had been excavated from the side of an esker – one of the long, sand-and-gravel ridges, formed from the beds of sub-glacial ice-age rivers, that are found snaking for miles across the Barren Ground. Using an axe, a trenching tool and a shovel, Critchell-Bullock and Hornby, with the help of two trappers, the Stewart brothers, had created a rectangular cavity of about ten by seven feet, and six feet six inches deep, in the lee side of the esker, sheltering it from the worst of the arctic winds. The walls were revetted with brushwood and moss in an attempt to prevent crumbling, and the brush roof, weighted with tons of gravel and sand, was supported by a ramshackle structure of bent and stunted branches scavenged from the area, which was sparse in timber. The door was accessed through a long snow tunnel and, with only a tiny window installed, practically no natural light was admitted. The interior of this cramping, snow-buried hut is well caught in Critchell-Bullock's pencil sketch. They had no plates or utensils apart from a frying pan and a few old gasoline tins. There were no shelves, no cupboards, no chairs or tables. The only 'furniture' consisted of the two men's beds, their cabin trunks and an old soap-box. The bunks were used not just for sleeping and sitting but as a butcher's block for skinning, gutting and cutting up meat and fish. It was a space hardly more comfortable than an enlarged wolf's den, and rather less well-appointed than a dug-out on the Somme.

The fact that Critchell-Bullock had been left alone that Christmas, to fall prey to his brooding and despair, seems indicative. Hornby himself had turned out to be incapable of staying put. Rather than devote time to fixing the house, or carefully cleaning the pelts they had trapped, he continually invented pretexts to disappear into the white void beyond the camp. He made futile, wide-ranging trips after caribou and firewood, trekked thirty miles down to the cabin of the Stewart brothers merely to pay his respects, or battled his way back to Reliance to fetch unnecessary items from a cache they had left there – only to return without them. But Critchell-Bullock's mood was complicated. He did indeed find it hard to cope without Hornby, but found it just as tough when he was present. In Edmonton the captain had loved and been inspired by the man. Not any more.

To Critchell-Bullock's tidy military sensibility, his partner's slovenly habits around camp were particularly repellent. He had become 'a white man who had largely gone native', a man who 'was prepared to live in squalor for longer periods than most'.

He never bathed or washed his hair. He declined to use hot water for his occasional ablutions, 'because hot water opens the pores and lets in the dirt'. He always used a stick for toilet paper, and he boasted that he had owned no underwear for twenty years.

Nor could Critchell-Bullock rely on Hornby for civilized talk. While he did not expect wit and amusement from trappers like the Stewarts, still less from the wandering Indian bands they occasionally met, he thought he could rely on Hornby to keep his mind responsive. But whenever they found themselves cabin-bound together above the Casba River, he no longer recognized the fascinating raconteur of their Edmonton days. Hornby refused to engage in serious conversation – at least as Critchell-Bullock conceived the term – but mainly confined himself to boasting and aggrandizement, opinionated theorizing and contrariness.

He was fond of making such pronouncements as: 'If I were King there would be no wars. There is no man living who could beat me in a straight fight. The Government ought to give me Artillery Lake as compensation for all the hardships I have endured on behalf of the North. The North has never known such a traveller as I. Hardships and the ability to starve like a gentleman are the only criteria of a good traveller. My name will live in history as I have made the greatest of all contributions to the North Country. I am the only white man with whom the Indians and Eskimos know they can safely leave their women.'

These caustic reflections were written a quarter-century after the events they describe, as a contribution to a projected *Encyclopaedia Arctica*. The essay is an overview of Hornby's life and legend, a piece which sets out to show its author undeceived by the Hornby myth. Yet Critchell-Bullock's overall tone is more often one of exasperated tolerance compared with the hatred and despair which occasionally overflow into his diary.

But the diary is by no means all bile and self-pity and, after the depth of winter passes, its mood gradually lightens with the lengthening days. There are further outbursts of complaint, but Christmas Eve's entry is the nadir of Critchell-Bullock's disappointment. After it, the text becomes more realistic, as he is driven to accept the Barrens – and his companion – on their own terms. He now knows that Hornby is not the genius he had thought he was. But with that insight come renewed (if occasional and fleeting) moments of good fellowship, humour, courage and achievement.

It had turned out to be a good winter for trapping, with the valuable white fox especially plentiful. They made four hundred fox and wolf pelts, which they proposed to take out by dog sled and then, as the snow and ice disappeared, by canoe, following the almost unprecedented seven-hundred-mile route down the Thelon River to Hudson Bay. But the Thelon was a daunting proposition. It had been descended by white men on only four or five previous occasions, none of them transporting such a heavy load of furs.

Time was pressing. They had to reach Hudson Bay before the freeze-up or else spend a futile winter at Chesterfield Inlet. So now, in June, they set off to find a short-cut to the great river by striking due east from the Casba. For several weeks they were lost. A series of violent blizzards forced them repeatedly into shelter and, whenever the weather cleared and they could travel, they found the snow mushy, or else too thinly crusted, which made transporting the canoes by sled maddeningly difficult. The dogs were practically useless for the task and so they man-hauled, having no choice, as melting ice continued to clog the lakes and streams until the end of June.

Matters improved as stretches of open water appeared in front of them. But the map – an original by the explorer J. W. Tyrrell, given to Jack in photostat by his friend George Douglas – was difficult to interpret and, in spite of discovering a fine eminence and naming it Mount Hornby, the two men were miserable, argumentative and unable to locate the main river channel because of the extraordinary stillness of the water in a flat land almost without drainage. They found themselves on a long reach of water unknown to the maps (they named it the Critchell-Bullock Arm), which presumably led to the Hanbury, but they could not determine how far away it was or in which direction.

Meanwhile their dogs were intractable; even Jack's Whitey, usually a paragon, did not behave as he should. Once one of their canoes sank and had to be salvaged. Another time Jack fell through thin ice and nearly drowned.

Blizzards persisted, sweeping down from the north, pinning them to their flimsy tents for days on end. At such times Critchell-Bullock occupied himself with his nature notes, or by taking and developing what he hoped would be money-spinning wildlife movies. Hornby, meanwhile, fluctuated between silence and compulsive talking. In his talkative moods he would provoke Critchell-Bullock into arguments about religion, war, the perfect desert island, or the ideal dinner. Hornby's gourmet ideas were noticeably sparer than Critchell-Bullock's, but he was truly provocative in his chosen island solitude. While the captain dreamed of Bermuda or the Seychelles, Hornby picked out the bleak isle of Rockall in the North Atlantic, 'because it would never breed any noxious insects' and 'it could be depended on to look after itself in the matter of general sanitation as a good rainstorm would wash everything away'.

Then at last, in the thunderous annual commotion that heralds sub-Arctic summer, the ice broke and they were able to enter the Thelon by canoe. But for the first 150 miles they met a grim succession of rapids, as long as two and a half miles. Some of these they risked running, but many had to be portaged, with the gear humped in packs by the dogs and the men – including the cabin trunks and the smaller of the canoes – to skirt the rapids. This required eight loads each before they were ready to walk the large canoe down on a line – very dangerous work, involving back-breaking strain along sheer banks and within easy slipping distance of the murderously racing water.

Their problems multiplied and resources dwindled. The canoes leaked and had to be repeatedly beached and unloaded for baling. Critchell-Bullock, while chopping wood, drove the axe into his toes, almost severing them. Hornby's final pair of moccasins disintegrated and he continued barefoot. Gasoline from one of the lamps contaminated the last of the flour, which they ate regardless. They were often hungry. What they craved was the rush of well-being given by the rich nourishment of the caribou's back-fat, tongue and raw bone-marrow. If they killed caribou meat they gorged, but invariably had more than they could eat or carry. Then on the next day, or perhaps the one after, they had no meal at all. Or they had fish. Too often their supplies ran only to putrid trout flesh, which gave them dysentery.

One by one the starving, exhausted dogs perished. Critchell-Bullock had destroyed his own favourite, Bhaie, months before, when he saw that the creature's frostbitten foot could never heal. Now the last and strongest of the dogs, Hornby's faithful Whitey, was also put to death. Both men knew that they, too, could quite easily die. Their weakness might lead to some catastrophic accident – a broken limb, a fractured skull, an infected wound. Or it could simply overwhelm them like a narcotic and take away the will to survive. That had nearly happened to Hornby in his cabin, Fort Hornby, near Fort Reliance, in 1921. He liked to tell how he had prepared his own coffin and tomb, and was actually lying in it when the Indian group that had been stealing from his fish-hooks all winter came in and fed him.

But this time there was no chance of outside intervention. Neither Indians nor trappers camped along the Thelon. However, eventually, after weeks of continual rapids, adverse winds and tempestuous currents, the water spread and calmed beneath their canoes and they entered the chain of lakes which make up the lower Thelon. Here, between Beverley and Aberdeen lakes, they saw an Eskimo camp: their first human contact for four months. They stopped to trade some tobacco for a pair of caribou tongues. The Eskimo spoke neither English nor French, but Hornby remembered a few phrases of their language.

He learned of a newly established Hudson's Bay Company trading post on Baker Lake. This was some 150 miles downstream, but much nearer than the settlement they had been aiming for, Chesterfield Inlet, which was 350 miles away. It is impossible to know if the spent couple would have made that extra 200 miles. Instead, two weeks later, they wearily paddled their overloaded, unbalanced canoes towards the Baker Lake landing stage, where a startled watcher called out from the shore, 'Where the hell have you two sprung from?'

'Edmonton,' said Hornby succinctly.

This was Hornby's dividend – the only one that ultimately he wanted. In that moment of laconic triumph all the toil, the hunger and the suffering seemed worthwhile. Despite his ill-judged risk-taking and treacherous luck, he had brought Critchell-Bullock and himself out. He was vindicated.

Critchell-Bullock, however, was hoping for a more tangible return on his investment. Even in his moments of deepest misery, he had always been able to cling to the thought that the trip would at least produce a healthy profit. After all, he had cinematic pictures of unexplored country, and he had furs. So it was a shattering blow to realize, as he soon did, how illusory these hopes were. The films would in due course turn out to be poorly photographed and of little commercial value. That, at least, was his fault. But when he and Hornby untied their fur sacks at Chesterfield Inlet, it was to find that every beautiful pelt had been ruined by the combined effects of damp and incompetent cleaning. The furs were a total loss and as a result Critchell-Bullock was cleaned out. In this case there was no one to blame but the legendary frontiersman himself.

It is a fair assumption that the loss did not much trouble Jack Hornby. He despised the money with which his family was so well provided and, though he was prepared to play civilization's game when it suited him, he never took material possessions seriously. Hornby also affected a complete lack of concern about his own future. Improvisation and luck had always guided him before and he saw no reason why they should not continue to do so.

2. Boyhood Heroes

On 23 July 1925, as Hornby and Critchell-Bullock watched a mass migration of at least two thousand caribou moving along the south shore of the Thelon, a very ordinary public schoolboy in southern England was approaching the end of his school career. In a few days he would leave the cocoon of school for ever, but first the tall, blond-haired teenager was to compete in the end-of-year swimming trials – his event, the long-distance freestyle race. His name was Edgar Christian and he was Jack Hornby's first cousin.

Edgar had been born on 6 June 1908. His father, Frank, was an artillery officer and, like all soldiers' families, the Christians had wandered from posting to posting. In 1919, a more permanent home was acquired, Bron Dirion, close to the sea in North Wales. This was where Edgar became a swimmer, seeking to toughen himself up in the chilly waters of nearby Caernarvon Bay.

Edgar's schooling took place beside another sea shore, the English Channel. He had started at the Grange School in Shorncliffe Road, Folkestone, a typical boys' private preparatory school of the time. In moulding Edgar's character, the school was quite as important as his family, and very deliberately so. The formation of character, not the development of the intellect, was seen as the primary function of the English prep school as it was then conceived.

The Grange had fifty boys and a staff of nine. They lived under the care of the bachelor headmaster, C. H. Wodeman, and a uniformed matron, Miss Young – the most important female presence in the building. Cyril Wodeman, at forty, had commitment, energy and animation, not all of it channelled into his job. His driving passion was for the works of Gilbert and Sullivan and, hard though it is to imagine in the prim and aquiline figure who looks out from the 1921 school photograph, Wodeman spent much of his spare time capering around on the amateur stage as Nanky Poo or the Lord High Executioner.

Deposited at the age of eight or nine in this austere institution, Edgar must have been puzzled at first by the collection of unusual characters to be found there, a proportion of whom were damaged veterans of the Great War. Many staff at such schools were good, even excellent teachers, but the minimum requirement was to be able to describe yourself, however loosely, as a gentleman. Eccentricity in its most general sense was rife, but boys quickly accustomed themselves even to the most unpredictable of these men.

On reaching thirteen, Edgar hoped to graduate to Marl-borough College, joining his brother Charles. But the full Marlborough fees were high enough at £125 10s to make a scholarship necessary, which was beyond Edgar. Instead, he stayed on modestly at the Grange until the age of fifteen, the school's upper limit, before moving a few miles east to Dover College as a day boy, for which the annual charges amounted to just twenty-one guineas. It is unclear where Edgar lived whilst at Dover. It is quite possible that he remained, by arrangement, under the care of Cyril Wodeman and his staff, living at the Grange and commuting the seven miles to Dover each day by tram or train.

The new school lacked the status of a grand old foundation like Rugby or Winchester, but was recognized all the same as a *bona fide* public school. Founded in 1871, it had aimed from the start, according to information printed in *The Times*, to send boys into the armed services, the Colonial Service, the Indian Army or the Burmese police, and such a prospectus, still in force half a century later, would have chimed perfectly with Colonel Christian's aspirations for his son. The headmaster, W. S. Lee, known as 'Piggy' or 'Stinker', had been in post since 1915 and was an advocate of Muscular Christianity. This anti-intellectual interpretation of the Christian message emphasized salvation through vigorous physical activity and the cultivation of 'pluck'. It had been the dominant ideology behind the last fifty years of British Imperialism.

Although the masters were better educated than at Folkestone, life at Dover College was continuous with what Edgar had known. Only in the system of discipline did it differ. As prefects, senior Dovorians ruled the juniors in everything outside the classroom, including administering the cane, in the belief that early authority instilled confidence and a sense of duty. The school's motto was – and is – *Non recuso laborem*: I refuse no work. But Edgar never had the chance to refuse the rank of Prefect. He was never offered it.

He knew he had been a perennial under-achiever. His friend Clement Park-Johnstone later remembered a remark of Edgar's during their last hours at school together. 'Well, I have not done anything here that I shall be remembered by!' Despite the intensive training in moral character, team activities, leadership and cheerfulness, Edgar still lacked the solid basis from which he might launch himself as a man into the world. But, as the school magazine recorded, that last swimming tournament gave him a rare taste of triumph. Summoning every ounce of determination, he held on to win the race, leading all the way and forging ahead in the last length to repel a determined counter-attack from his own house captain, Bradford. His performance in that test of endurance was enough to secure for his House the school Swimming Cup. For a few hours, at least, Edgar knew what it was to be a hero.

Edgar's notions about heroism were quite unexceptional for his time, and were probably formed long before he came to Dover College. But his five terms there threw up two notable events that massively endorsed them.

Throughout the first half of 1924, the schoolboys of England had excitedly followed the progress of General Bruce's Imperial Expedition to climb Mount Everest. Some subscribed to a special offer of philatelic covers, the stamps franked at the Tibetan base camp. All revered the figure of Bruce's star climber, the Charterhouse schoolmaster George Leigh Mallory, who had provided the newspapers with a magnificently insouciant reason for attempting the world's highest mountain: 'Because it is there.'

Great was the dismay, therefore, when it was learned that this hero had died during a final assault on the summit. On 8 June, two days after Edgar's sixteenth birthday, Mallory and his partner Andrew Irvine had been glimpsed from far below, two specks in the snow moving strongly upwards to within a few hundred feet of their objective. Neither man would be seen again until Mallory's body was discovered in 1999 lying two thousand feet below the summit. Perhaps they had reached their goal before perishing on the way down – even now, the evidence is inconclusive. But, for Edgar and his generation, faith in Mallory's success was incidental to the bigger cult of his heroism.

If Mallory had indeed died returning from the summit, his fate could be seen as a vertical equivalent to Robert Scott's journey to the South Pole twenty-four years earlier. A remarkable lecture on Captain Scott, who at that time still perched unchallenged on the highest echelon of British heroism, had been heard at the school in Edgar's second term. Given by Captain E. R. Evans, R.N., it was a 'most moving and interesting' talk, illustrated with a 'large and interesting selection of excellent slides'.

Evans's appearance in a community like Dover College was calculated to create a small sensation. He was the most senior survivor of the expedition and, with Scott, had crossed the Great Ice Barrier, ascended the Beardmore Glacier and travelled across the polar plateau to within 150 miles of the Pole. Luckily (for him) he was not picked for the final polar run, but had nevertheless almost died from scurvy and exhaustion while retracing his steps to base. He was saved by the heroics of Chief Stoker Lashly and Petty Officer Crean, who brought him in.

Evans might have reminded Edgar of one of his prep school masters. This brash, vivid, unpredictable naval officer was too excitable and tactless to earn Scott's unqualified trust. But his love of horseplay revealed a wide streak of childishness (he later became the author of several adventure stories for juvenile readers) which – combined with his unquestioned membership of Scott's pantheon – would have made Evans an irresistible draw at any school. In Dover he also had a more local fame as a war hero, which for a while had made him the darling of the whole country. As 'Evans of the *Broke*' he had commanded a vessel in the Dover Patrol which had attacked a German G42 destroyer bombarding Dover Harbour. Evans released torpedoes and then, in Nelsonian style, rammed and grappled with the G42, sustaining forty casualties in ferocious hand-to-hand combat. Evans is reputed to have shouted at the Kaiser's sailors, swimming around him in the oily swell, 'Remember the *Lusitania!*'

Evans remained (in public at least) ever loyal to the Scott cult, but did not gloss over the mistakes made in the South. It was obvious that if the final push had started earlier and moved faster, it would have succeeded. But in an effort to spare his ponies, Scott had delayed until the end of the Antarctic winter, using up precious non-renewable resources of food and fuel and making his death by starvation on the return from the Pole almost inevitable. Amundsen's contrasting success with dogs, Evans told the boys, proved beyond doubt that huskies, with their greater tolerance of cold, were superior to either ponies or man-hauling. There was all the more reason therefore to praise Scott. Struggling cheerfully against impossible odds, he had made eight hundred miles to the pole and another six hundred back.

The tale of Evans's own near death in the snow was in itself a paradigm of heroism in action. Crippled by scurvy, he had several times begged Lashly and Crean to leave him 'in my sleeping bag, with what food they could spare'. They had refused. Finally, with Evans unable to go on, Crean had continued alone to fetch relief if he could, while Lashly remained with his officer. After two days they heard dogs, and moments later a husky poked its nose through the flap of the tent and licked Evans's face. 'I put my poor weak hands up and gripped his furry ears. Perhaps to hide my feelings I kissed his old hairy Siberian face, with the kiss that was meant for Lashly.'

Such words were poetry to the ears of boys brought up on juvenile weekly papers such as *The Boy's Own Paper*, *The Magnet* and *Pluck*, as well as adventure stories by R. M. Ballantyne, G. A. Henty and Gordon W. Stables. In the way that they illustrated the same British grit, the real-life tragedies of Scott and Mallory overlapped with those fictional worlds in the public's perception to create a composite account of what made a man. These boys' imaginations had been trained to respond especially to images of the frozen lands as ideal theatres for trial and courage, because their severe beauty brought one closer to the sublime truth of creation and the mind of God. In such places, conflict with the elements provided the greatest fulfilment. Even apparent failure could transform itself into a higher form of success and spiritual renewal.

Virtually all boyhood reading underlined this message: the truly heroic thing is often to endure and yet to fail; to face disaster and not be found wanting; to Play the Game. That spirit, Edgar knew, was what his mother Marguerite's famous cricketing uncle, Albert Neilson Hornby, had epitomized. It was also, even more surely, what the cricketer's youngest son, the glamorous Jack, was all about.

The Hornbys were Lancashire cotton magnates from Blackburn who set themselves up as country squires near the Cheshire town of Nantwich. Marguerite's grandfather leased a large property with eighty acres and sent his sons from there to Harrow to complete the transformation. The last of these sons was Marguerite's father Charles; the penultimate was A. N. Hornby, the celebrated sportsman and 'cricketing squire'. Just five foot two inches and known on this account as Monkey, he had in 1864 and 1865 played for Harrow against Eton in front of 16,000 spectators. He went on to represent the Gentlemen against the Players at Lords and to captain Lancashire to its first county championship. In 1882, he led England in the year's only test match against Australia, later celebrated as the 'Ashes' test. On the last day of play, a crowd of 40,000 watched tensely as the captain, the smallest player ever witnessed at the Oval Cricket Ground, opened the batting for England's second innings with Dr W. G. Grace.

Fiercely attacked by the bowling of the 'Demon' Spofforth, England lost by seven runs in one of the most exciting finishes to a test match so far seen. English disappointment was expressed in a mock In Memoriam notice in the *Sporting Times*, informing readers that the ashes of the English game would be taken to Australia. But Hornby's reputation survived the defeat. Though he himself had been clean bowled in the test by Spofforth for just nine runs, his aura as 'the Pocket Hercules', one of the sporting idols of the age, was undiminished. He was an agile, risk-taking, exciting exponent of the imperial game and his record score off a single stroke – ten, all run – still stands. Hornby led Lancashire County until the age of fifty-two, but he had also captained England at rugby, played soccer for Blackburn Rovers, and all his life ridden fearlessly to hounds. As if all this were not enough, he appears in some lines by Francis Thompson which are among the most delicately melancholic ever written about a sport:

> *It is little I repair to the matches of the Southron folk,*
> *Though my own red roses there may blow;*
> *It is little I repair to the matches of the Southron folk,*
> *Though the red roses crest the caps I know,*
> *For the field is full of shades as I near the shadowy coast*
> *And a ghostly batsman plays to the bowling of a ghost*
> *And I look through my tears on a soundless-clapping host*
> *As the run-stealers flicker to and fro,*
> *To and fro: –*
> *O my Hornby and my Barlow long ago!*

By 1925, it was indeed long ago. A. N. Hornby was eighty and ailing, a fall from his hunter having confined him to a bath-chair. Tales of his batting must undoubtedly have fired up young Edgar from time to time, especially when he himself put on white flannels. Yet it was John Hornby – Edgar's mother's favourite cousin Jack – who had a more immediate hold on the boy's imagination.

Marguerite Christian, the same age as her cousin, had always delighted in Jack. His smallness and restless enthusiasm brought out something in her that perhaps went beyond cousinly affection. But, unlike conventional first cousins, Marguerite and Jack possessed the same genes on both sides, since Charles and Albert Hornby had each married a daughter of the publishing magnate Sir William Ingram. With this double consanguinity, any juvenile thoughts of romance between them were swiftly suppressed.

Edgar had never met Jack – at least not since he was a small boy – but news of Jack's escapades had been filtering back to England since before the Great War. As a modern embodiment of frontier survival skills and general hardiness – a man at ease with Eskimo and Red Indian, husky dog and canoe, carbine and spring-trap – it would be hard to beat Jack. As an Englishman of impeccable breeding, with the added lustre of the Military Cross to show for his war service, he perfectly fitted the stereotype of the British hero that was found in the pages of boys' fiction. Edgar must many times have boasted to schoolfellows about his remarkable cousin, and many times fantasized that, one day, he would join him on the open trail.

With Edgar's poor academic record, his immediate prospects in the world, as he quit Dover College, were limited. For him there was no chance of prolonging his academic education at a prestigious institution such as Oxford University or the 'Shop' – the Woolwich Military Academy. If he had had a slightly better head on his shoulders, he might have been articled as a clerk or placed on one of the lower rungs of the banking ladder. But an immature young man of no great intellect or savvy was generally thought most suitable for the colonial life. Kenya, New Zealand or Canada beckoned.

Edgar was sent in autumn 1925 to work at a market garden near High Wycombe in Buckinghamshire. If he was to farm in the colonies, he would need some technical and economic knowledge, the type of education that the public schools rarely took seriously. Whether he absorbed any useful information does not appear in his surviving writings, but at any rate he stayed at Wycombe until late autumn, when he heard the news of Great Uncle Hornby's illness in Nantwich. It seemed serious and, if A. N. Hornby died, Jack would surely return to England for the funeral. It would be Edgar's chance, at last, to get to know his revered cousin.

3. Finest Sons

A. N. Hornby had been laid low by a catastrophic stroke at
the end of November 1925. Jack and Critchell-Bullock were
writing their reports in Ottawa, after a laborious sea
and rail journey from Hudson Bay via Halifax and Montreal.
Critchell-Bullock was compiling a book-length report, 'An
Expedition of Biological Research to Sub-Arctic Canada,
1924–5', while Jack was at work on a rather slimmer collection of notes for the government on caribou and musk-
oxen. He was still enjoying the afterglow of their escape
from the Barrens but, as this sombre family news reached
him, the euphoria drifted away. He hastily wrapped up his
writing – in finished form the notes ran to only sixteen closely
typed pages – and made immediate arrangements to travel
home.

It was Jack's third visit to Nantwich in twenty-one years.
He was not exactly the Prodigal Son – he had last been seen
at home in 1924 – but there were distinct similarities. A
wealthy mother had indulgently underwritten his wasteful
and aimless activities with remittances of cash, if not encouragement. And, like the Prodigal Son, Jack had suffered
famine, and had on several occasions come within a hair's
breadth of death by starvation. But he was no degenerate.
While he indulged in a little riotous living on occasion,
his true leaning had always been towards asceticism – the

rejection of the comfort and privilege of his background. He certainly did not come home to beg his parents' forgiveness.

Jack was the youngest of A. N. Hornby's four sons, two of whom were still alive. In physique, or lack of it, he took after his father to the extent that, in Canada, the Monkey nickname was also applied to him. He had followed family tradition by attending Harrow, where he had showed much of the old man's wiry athleticism, excelling in running, hurdling and fives and, with his 'india-rubber legs', winning the school sack race by a distance. However, his academic performance was not good enough to gain him a university place and he faced a common dilemma for the sons of Victorian wealth: the choice between the army and idleness. As the Boer War broke out, two of his brothers had taken the military option, one dying in South Africa, the other perishing in the Great War.

Meanwhile, the oldest brother, Albert, had chosen to follow his father as a sporting gentleman. But neither a distant African bloodbath nor a life in white flannels was Jack's idea of personal fulfilment. Nor did he relish the endless repetition of the Monkey's 1881 batting average, or being reminded that his father was the only man to have captained England at rugby and cricket in the same calendar year.

There had been family hopes, according to the account he gave Critchell-Bullock, of his joining the diplomatic service, but instead he had spent a footloose year or two in Germany. In the Black Forest, he fell for a beautiful but sceptical widow, who was older and several inches taller than himself. To impress the lady, Jack entered the long-distance ski championships and came in second, despite having no previous experience. As Critchell-Bullock related it, 'when this achievement failed to establish his eligibility, he threw in his hand and left for Canada'. This anecdote, which Critchell-Bullock heard during their long winter together in 1924–5, shows Jack behaving with just the kind of quixotic reckless-ness that would characterize his whole life. It also shows that he did not go to Canada a complete novice of the snows.

His decision in favour of Canada was based on a shrewd self-assessment. He knew that he would not be afraid of hardship, for he had already begun to understand his own delight in extremes. Perhaps he could already visualize him-self as 'the Hermit of the Arctic', punishing his body zealously like an early Christian ascetic. Not the least attractive aspect to this was that his father would find such a life completely incomprehensible. When, at the age of twenty-three, Jack finally bought a ticket for Halifax, Nova Scotia, and packed his bags, A. N. Hornby noted in the family album, with a terseness that left no room for emotion: 'Jack left home, April 7th 1904, for Canada.'

Almost twenty-two years later, and back at Parkfield, his parents' house, Jack felt out of place and behaved awkwardly. He could quite justifiably claim to be more used to the rough ways of a frontier camp than the social stratification of a Cheshire country home, where everyone spoke in the clipped accents of public school and gentry – except, that is, for the thirty-two indoor and outdoor servants. In this constrained atmosphere, things that needed to be said were left unsaid. At best, they were half-said. Emotion was translated into sentiment, contained by domestic ritual or channelled towards favourite animals and sport. Jack disliked all this.

'Here no one is sincere and I feel like an absolute stranger,' he wrote to George Douglas. 'I am like a wild animal caged.'

A. N. Hornby had clung stubbornly to life until, it seemed, the ordeal would never end. Then, on 17 December, within a few days of Jack's arrival, his father's innings ended. *The Times* carried a long obituary. For the funeral, during which it rained in a steady downpour, local people lined the route of the cortège, the working men of the town doffing their caps as the hearse drawn by plumed horses passed by. A poignant moment came after the body had been lowered into the ground. As the minister, the Reverend J. H. Armitstead, pronounced the phrase 'dust to dust', a single red rose was dropped on to the coffin. Someone had plucked it from an enormous wreath sent by the Lancashire County Cricket Club.

Jack was perfect at the graveside, comforting his mother and standing steadily with eyes cast down as his elder brother unfolded a sheet of paper and intoned:

> *It is little I repair to the matches of the Southron folk*
> *Though my own red roses there may blow . . .*

The voice continued on to the end of the poem, muted by gusts of wind and the sheeting rain.

The funeral was followed by a sense of anti-climax. The mourners dispersed. A week later came Christmas, but in Parkfield it seemed a leaden celebration. There was, in everything, the sense that an era had dwindled to an end.

For several weeks, Jack, with no particular ties or occupation, was busy with matters arising from his father's death. He did his best to be dutiful, but the business bored him and the houseful of women increased his restlessness. He loved Ada Hornby, but was having trouble coping with her emotional demands. 'Though I am fond of my mother and as you know consider her second to no woman, my life has always been with men,' he had written to Critchell-Bullock from England on a similar visit two years before.

As the New Year turned, the question in Nantwich was if and when Jack would return to Canada. Ada Hornby, a daughter of wealth in her own right and formidably determined, was used to having her way. She now began to bombard Jack with reasons why he should never go back. Two of her sons had died abroad – was he set on being the third? There was a large home and money for him at Nantwich and, besides, now that A. N. was gone she needed him more than ever. Was he determined to add filial abandonment to her widowhood?

In England, Jack would never want for money. Ada had set aside £10,000 for him in her will, as well as the proceeds of all her insurance policies (making a net sum of more than £1,000,000 in modern terms). And, apart from anything else, it was high time he married. If he didn't know where to look, he could do worse than cast his eye about this very house. Did he not have a widowed sister-in-law who was desperately in need of support and still attractive enough? Feeling hunted and vulnerable, he wrote to Critchell-Bullock:

At the present time I am in a very awkward position as my mother is alone and thinks I ought to stay with her.

She curiously thinks that money and an easy life are all
that one can wish for. Money, I admit, is all right but
the latter does not appeal to me.

Ada's entreaties and unwelcome suggestions were therefore
counter-productive, far more likely to drive Jack off than get
him to stay. There is some evidence that only a few weeks
before, back in Ottawa, he had begun to wonder if he should
give up the sub-Arctic and settle permanently in England. If
so, this thought began to evaporate in the presence of his
mother. He started thinking obsessively about the North
again – dreaming of snow and of caribou, assembling fantasy
outfits, enumerating the uncompleted objectives of his
Thelon journey with Critchell-Bullock. His life had always
been lived in rough country with men. Could he give it all
up for feminine comforts and idleness?

The tension between himself and his mother also restricted
his conversation. The only topics that reliably interested Jack
were related to his experiences in the Barren Lands, in
particular the more death-defying moments. But no mother
relishes tales of her son in danger, so it was a relief to them
both when he received invitations to the homes of people
who delighted in his yarns. In Shropshire he called on the
family of one of the first men he had travelled and hunted
with in the Barrens, a wealthy sportsman named Cosmo
Melvill, who had died in Edmonton from double pneumonia
five years earlier. Jack was able to talk to his heart's content
to the Melvill parents about the times with Cosmo, since this
was exactly why he had been asked to come. He also called
on some Ingram relations in Sheringham, Norfolk. The

Hornby family owned a holiday home in this seaside town and Jack may have taken his bereaved mother there for a rest. At all events, his five-year-old cousin, Perpetua Ingram, never forgot sitting on his knee at her home and being told:

> . . . stories about his travels which included a sighting of a mermaid. I questioned him about this (my father, being a realist, had told me they did not exist) but I still remember Jack saying, as he stroked my hair, 'I promise you that I have seen a mermaid.'

Shortly afterwards there was another invitation, sent by Marguerite Christian, from Bron Dirion. Jack jumped at this chance to see his cousin and her family in their own home and, some time in the first months of 1926, he made the journey to Caernarvon Bay. For five of the Christian children – Gwen, Charles, Fred, Dulcie and Rita – the visit would seem to have had no particular significance. But for the sixth, seventeen-year-old Edgar, it was momentous.

At Bron Dirion, the explorer was brimming with tales of the far North. All he needed was a listener and Edgar jumped at the role. Should Jack's flow at any time dry up, the boy would be ready with his prompting questions. Had Jack really walked hundreds of miles across snowfields? Did he ever cut holes in the river ice to catch trout? Had he shot a bear?

One year, 1918, Jack had in fact shot two: one at fifteen yards, another at five. The second time, he'd heard the bear during the night getting into his cache – his meat store. He'd grabbed his pistol, run out of the cabin in his underwear and almost bumped smack into the beast. He stepped back and shot him once through the nostril. The bullet ploughed through the brain-stem and the bear crashed down at Jack's feet, dead as a log.

This was spine-tingling stuff. But what Jack really loved to talk about were the caribou and the Indians. Spend even a short time with Indians and you appreciated that caribou – reindeer, in Edgar's terms – were the only game that really counted. They were easy enough to slaughter if you came upon a migration – Jack had sometimes seen the land 'black with caribou' – but in winter the individuals were scattered, reduced, and damnably difficult to find.

Quite apart from the meat, itself far superior to all other food sources in the Barrens, an Indian traditionally got almost everything he had from caribou. Jack could demonstrate how, from just one carcass and using no other tool but a knife, a canoe could be built. The ribs formed the struts of the curved frame and the hide made a waterproof outer skin, if properly tanned in a preparation of brain tissue. Sewing and pack thread was spun from the spinal sinews, dried, split and rolled on twigs. A strong twine – babiche – was made from braided strips of the hide. A paddle could be fashioned from caribou leather stretched over the antlers. Of course, these skills were fast becoming redundant. Hornby considered the natives today a sad sight, as they grew increasingly dependent on ready-made, white men's equipment.

Jack would disparage the modern Indians. He hated what he saw as their insatiable, atavistic lust for killing each and every animal they came across, which, since their adoption of rifles, had already virtually wiped out the musk-ox and would, he thought, one day do the same for wolf, bear and caribou. At the same time, he always acknowledged the debt he owed to his favourite tribe, the Indians of Great Bear Lake. With them he had first penetrated the land above the conifer forests that fringed the lake, the bare rolling tundra of the Barrens. He had learned to adopt the fluent, half-crouching, long-striding jog-trot which the Indian could keep up for hours, even across the roughest snow. As his friend Cosmo Melvill observed, with a touch of chagrin,

> There is no stalking or finesse about their hunting, they walk all animals up (except moose) and, when close, run at them. Hornby can keep up with them but personally I can't.

But Jack could not merely 'keep up' with the Indians, he could rise above them. He could see, as they could not, that their rifles would one day 'clean the land' of caribou and all other animals. The thought made him bitter at times, for as he said, 'without the caribou the charm of the Barrens would disappear'.

In evoking this charm for his young listener, Jack was at last off the conversational leash. He indulged his imagination to the full, felt his way back along the threads, lavished on his cousin all the hyperbole of the true obsessive. And Edgar's eyes were wide. He wished he could see it too.

Edgar thought things over. High Wycombe was dull. If he was really destined for the colonies, then so be it, but what could he learn in Buckinghamshire? Jack could teach him more in three minutes than he could learn at the market garden in three months. His Ingram grandmother, who was also Jack's Aunt Marguerite, was staying with them and Edgar confided in her. How, he asked, would his mother react if he wanted to go back to Canada with Jack for a trip? Edgar's grandmother was encouraging. She knew how much Jack and Marguerite meant to each other. She agreed to suggest the idea to her nephew and her daughter.

Jack was already persuaded that he could not stay in England, whatever Ada Hornby said. He had been mulling over what he could do if he did go back to Canada, but a limited number of ideas suggested themselves, each with drawbacks. Teaming up with other old hands left problems of precedence and Jack wasn't sure he could subordinate himself. But could he face the hell of another winter alone in a filthy dug-out or cabin, suffering sub-zero temperatures and with too little food? Now, unexpectedly, here was a new option. He liked Edgar and was attracted by the idea of introducing a new generation into the Barrens, to show him the musk-oxen before they died out, and let him see one of the last true wildernesses before modern man overwhelmed it *en masse*.

Marguerite, too, was enthusiastic about the idea, and so it was a united front that put the idea to Colonel Christian, in barracks at Portsmouth. If Edgar wanted to go to Canada, and his grandmother and mother couldn't see why he shouldn't, and Jack wanted to take him, why should Colonel Christian object? He did not, agreeing with his wife and mother-in-law, not implausibly, that such a trip would wake Edgar up and toughen him. There was also a background factor which played a part in the decision. England was going through a time of worrying social instability. There was unrest in the industrial areas and a miners' strike was looming, threatening fuel shortages. The stock market might be affected and there were even predictions of a revolutionary uprising. It seemed a good time for a boy to have the true values of loyalty, family and comradeship reinforced in a clean and faraway environment.

All was settled within a matter of days. Jack returned to Nantwich to inform Ada, in what must have been a tight-lipped interview, that he had agreed to take her great-nephew Edgar to Canada for his education and could hardly go back on his word. Passages to Montreal were booked on the SS *Montrose*, owned by the Canadian Pacific Railway company. Friends in Canada were informed by letter or cable of Jack's imminent arrival. Packing commenced.

Before assembling his personal outfit, Edgar would have consulted with Jack. But his cousin is likely to have been of little help to him. The details of packing an outfit in advance – sorting items into such categories as Essential, Useful and Not Wanted – was never of much interest to him. So Edgar packed what he thought he might need, including small presents from his sisters and a New Testament and Book of Common Prayer from his mother. Then he did the rounds to say good-bye to friends in the village: the part-time postman William Williams, the schoolmaster Llewellyn Parry, and John Davies, the vicar of St Beuno's church, where Colonel Christian used to read the lesson for the 11 a.m. English-language service. Finally, it was off to

Nantwich to collect Jack, and then by car the short distance
to Crewe station, where the adventurers would catch the
boat train.

They missed the connection. It caused Edgar to hop
around the platform with impatience and concern, in case
they should also miss their sailing. But Jack was imperturb-
able, simply smiling and saying quietly that, if necessary,
they would catch the next. Edgar was struck by this simple
demonstration of Jack's indifference to Bradshaw's Railway
Guide and other protocols regulating 'civilized' life. The
careless, impulsive side of Jack's character, insofar as it
appeared to either Edgar or his parents, seemed an endearing
quality, and the question of where it might lead under extreme
circumstances did not at first enter their heads. When Edgar
said good-bye to his family and his home, it was with
complete confidence that he would return unscathed, after
passing through many thrilling adventures.

When the train from Crewe finally delivered the travellers
to Liverpool, the SS *Montrose* was still alongside. She sailed
on Monday, 19 April 1926.

Military duty had prevented Colonel Christian from seeing
Edgar off. At Clarence Barracks, Portsmouth, he had written
a farewell letter to his son which contained a realistic assessment of the journey ahead, as if advancing a corrective to
Jack's easy insouciance and Edgar's innocent enthusiasm.

Just a few lines to say goodbye & to wish you, with
my heart, all success in your great adventure.
Remember our trust and love go with you. You have

ambition & I am sure you will overcome all difficulties. You will have great hardships probably, but be patient and work hard.

Always try & do right no matter what others may think. You are out to lay the foundation of your life.

Edgar apparently replied in a bubbly letter, full of heady optimism for the coming months. In a second letter which his son received in Canada, the Colonel again sought to caution him, more firmly this time, against over-confidence:

Remember we think of you with hope & love & I know you look forward to success. But life is full of disappointments & disillusionment & things very seldom turn out as we hope. Nothing is gained which is worth having & which can give us real joy & peace, without hard work, renunciation & sacrifice & patience. We can do nothing ourselves without God's help & this we must pray for.

This letter carries the first scintilla of anxiety about how Jack's expedition with Edgar had been framed. But any possible fears on Frank Christian's part were soothed by his belief that true character emerged only from adversity and that an English gentleman always came through — articles of faith that were integral to his military ethic and his brand of Christianity.

In this letter, Edgar's father also expressed a practical hope: that the expedition be chronicled. 'Try,' he urged, 'to keep a sort of diary of your life till you come back.'

4. Feast

Despite the age difference of almost thirty years, Edgar found himself much enjoying his cousin's company on *Montrose*.

> The more I get to know Jack the nicer he seems to be & his extraordinary knowledge on some subjects is really wonderful considering how long he has been living so far away from civilization.
>
> It is a great pleasure having someone like Jack to travel with. Being an old traveller by the C.P.R. he is recognized and looked up to by the Stewards on the boat and consequently he gets the best attentions from the Saloon Stewards who waited on him before and [they] have even got leave from the Head Steward to change tables in order to get his table.

Jack undoubtedly had startling charisma for such a boy. Edgar, so deeply impressed already by Jack's exploits in the wilderness, now saw his cousin in the appearance of a complete man of the world, at ease in the first-class lounge and at the captain's table, his portmanteau furnished with all the appropriate clothing, including the dinner jacket and dress shirt which Jack carried with him at all times.

Though he seemed to understand and play the social game faultlessly, the quality that placed him, in Edgar's eyes, beyond the reach of criticism was his apartness. He was a lone wolf who knew the law of the jungle well enough to ignore it, if he chose. If he also carried with him a freight of superstitions and obsessions that, even to a friendly eye, must have marked him out as a true oddball – and a man who at times came dangerously close to insanity – this was not apparent to Edgar. His hero-worship of Jack was blind.

The ship in which they sailed had made her maiden voyage only four years previously and, powered by engines equipped with double-reduction gears, she could make sixteen or seventeen knots. Travelling first class, Edgar and Jack had the pick of accommodation available to the cabin passengers.

The trip across seems to be an absolute luxury & like a week in a London hotel. Everything is wonderfully fitted up and the grub cannot be improved on I am sure. Yesterday the weather was not any too good & lots of people were ill but I took Jacks tip and kept on walking about the deck. I shan't mind if it comes rough now as I feel I have got my sea legs & have felt very fit. To walk around the deck 8 or 9 times is a mile long and so although I dont get Enough Exercise I must walk several miles a day.

There are 288 Cabin passengers and a thousand third class of whom about 50 are young barnardo boys.

The voyage ended on 25 April with Edgar's first experience of troublesome Canadian ice. They had encountered icebergs at sea and now the St Lawrence River was unusually frozen, making it necessary for an icebreaker to clear a channel as far as Quebec. But, unusually for the time of year, Montreal itself remained icebound and to get there they transferred to the Canadian Pacific Railway. It was the first leg of a rail journey which would eventually stretch for more than a thousand miles.

Next morning, 26 April, they pulled into Montreal, and Jack reserved rooms at the Windsor Hotel. Just as he always travelled first class when in civilization, he took care to stay at the best hotels. Overlooking Dominion Square, the Windsor was a palatial establishment of seven storeys, an imposing height in that era.

Writing to his father, Edgar was delighted with everything he saw.

> In many ways this City seems better than London. The streets are much wider and are not crowded with top-decked buses. The Tram service beats England into a Cocked Hat. They are much Longer Cars and hold more passengers and travel at double the speed with not so much rattling and shaking.

The sophistication of the transport system was not all that caught the young man's eye.

> There is one thing which strikes me more than anything else here and that is the girls and women. I am not getting smitten or anything like that but for beauty I dont wish to see any better. They are not quite as tall

as the average young girl in England but for a good figure and prettiness I have never seen one in England to equal them. Yesterday we went to a Cafeteria & a girl of about twenty-one came in while we were there & there must be lots in England who would have paid to see her but nobody took any particular notice and she did not seem a bit conceited and in fact struck me as if quite unaware of her own beauty. The feminine dress is to my mind much better than English. Jack says it is French style but whatever it is it is very neat and tidy.

Although Jack took Edgar to a picture-house one evening ('there is no smoking which makes it much nicer to see anything on the screen'), the time available for frivolity was limited. Jack was keen to get on to Ottawa and, in the meantime, he wanted to call on 'various people in the town'. Among these was what Edgar calls:

an old-timer who spent many days trapping with [Jack] years ago and to hear them talk of the good old days and how they spent their well-earned money was an Education in itself.

This was the first of several introductions to old hands of the North and, with each one, Edgar became more impressed with his cousin's standing in the élite group of men who had lived close to the Arctic Circle. Jack, the old Harrovian and *habitué* of first-class travel and the best hotels, was accepted not only by travellers and explorers but by the true professionals, the fur-trappers, whose livelihood was won in naked confrontation with nature and the elements.

Dazzled by Jack's status among these men, Edgar missed the critical undertones of their conversations. Or perhaps they remained suppressed in his presence. But the fact is that some of the old-timers were wondering just what Jack Hornby thought he was doing, taking this babe into the Barrens. Jack, however, was careful not to announce any too specific plans. He varied his accounts of how far north he intended going and what his objectives were, creating a shifting target for the misgivings of others. This tactic makes it difficult to assess whether or not Jack had himself, at this stage, settled such questions in his own mind.

Jack was much happier allowing conversation to veer off into the past, full of anecdotes and folklore. Edgar noticed how some of Jack's friends would press him to write up 'all his trips and adventures with Eskimos'. Jack explained that 'it is of no interest to him because he has known them for so long', a cue for the stories to flow again: tales of his experiences in the far North and the lessons he had learned in native ways in the Barrens. In this way, Edgar began to piece together a picture of Jack's early journeys into the territory to which he, in turn, was soon to be introduced.

After two days in Montreal, with Edgar helping himself to a few sheets of the Windsor Hotel's headed notepaper, they checked out. The next stage on the Canadian Pacific Railway was the capital city, Ottawa, where they arrived on Friday 30 April, registering at the Château Laurier. Of all the hotels they used during this journey, only the Laurier still stands.

Built in 1912 and modelled on a Loire château, it was also the most luxurious, boasting a private bathroom for every spacious bedroom, magnificent Tiffany stained-glass windows in the lobby and splendid moulded ceilings to all the public rooms. The walls were lined with the mounted heads of Canada's big game and Jack pointed out to Edgar the individual species – the horned buffalo and bearded musk-ox, the grimacing brown bear and the antlered caribou – which were so important to those extracting a living from the frozen North.

The Laurier provided an extreme contrast to Jack's stone-age accommodation above the Casba River during his last winter in the North. 'Feast and famine,' Jack would say simply if Edgar commented on the Laurier's luxury. He was referring to the title of his work-in-progress about the Barren Lands, *In the Land of Feast and Famine*. The phrase summed up a strategy of survival in the Barren Ground, which Jack had learned from the Indians themselves. With lean times rarely more than a day or two away in the Barrens, you gorge yourself to the limit when you get the chance. In the same spirit, the feather mattresses and cream teas of the Laurier should be enjoyed, for what was to follow might be a comfortless snow-hole, thirty miles from a tree and a thousand from the nearest street-car.

As soon as they had settled in, a meeting was set up with Guy Blanchet, a government surveyor who lived in Ottawa. He and Jack had first met in 1906 and then again, more significantly, in 1922 on Great Slave Lake. Blanchet had been engaged on a survey, from his boat *Ptarmigan*, of the complicated pattern of islands and coastline at the east end of the lake, and had met Jack coming out after another winter on short rations, 'more or less starving'. Jack was, however, of service to Blanchet, showing him a new channel and making a sketch-map which proved to be surprisingly helpful. Later, near Fort Resolution, Blanchet suggested that Jack join his party, but the offer was turned down and Jack went ashore. In a letter written years later, Blanchet described Jack's extraordinary subsequent behaviour:

> The wind was rising again and finally I decided to pull out and run for shelter behind Moose Island. We had hardly started when H rushed to the shore and jumped into a skiff. I ran to Mission Island and anchored in poor shelter. H arrived after a tough row and when he came alongside he said, 'I can't go but I wanted to give you a fish' . . . All this was characteristic of H. He meant well but did such foolish things.

Edgar and Jack's stay in Ottawa lasted four days, during which they played golf with Blanchet, Edgar much admiring the well-appointed club-house. They also took a canoe, starting from the Rideau Canal beside the hotel and paddling several miles up the Ottawa River. Edgar marvelled, as he was no doubt intended to do, at the canoeing skills of the two men.

Blanchet and Jack discussed their various plans. The surveyor was just about to leave for the North on a carefully conceived mapping expedition through Lake Athabaska to the Dubawnt River. What, he wanted to know, were Jack's intentions? The answer threw up a confusing variety of options, summarized by Edgar in his first letter home:

The plans now are to go on to Edmonton and get fixed up, to go out north and settle in for Winters Trapping in The Great Slave lake district. We are first making for Fort Smith where he will prospect as he goes through and sees if there is any mineral or oil to be found.

This time Jack says he is going to live more in Comfort if he can because he has plenty of time on hand and will take plenty of provisions and stores.

Blanchet was concerned about the confusion here. How far would Jack and Edgar go into the Barren Ground? And were they trapping or prospecting? Jack had been talking mysteriously about 'some claims of his where silver mining is being started at Fort Smith', but would not elaborate. In any event, Blanchet, after meeting Edgar, thought it essential that Jack did not go north without adequate food and equipment. He offered transportation by boat as far as he himself was going, and help from his gang to move Jack's outfit over the portages. Jack temporized. They would meet, he said, in Edmonton to discuss the details, but meanwhile he had to continue on to Toronto without delay.

During the long rail journeys between cities, Edgar had Jack to himself and could badger him with questions about his life in the North. Every encounter with an old-timer had yielded new details of his cousin's biography and this was a chance to fill in the gaps. It is impossible to tell how much of his early years Jack confided to Edgar. There was little, probably, about the war and plenty about the Indians and Eskimo, and the time spent around Dease Bay on Great Bear Lake with Cosmo Melvill. This pre-war period was Jack's happiest. It was when he had first encountered the French missionary fathers, and when he'd lived sporadically and in great contentment – though scandalizing the priests – with an Indian woman, Arimo. This was also when he'd met one of his greatest friends in the North, an affable and intelligent mining engineer named George Douglas. The two had corresponded ever since, and Douglas was perhaps the one man in Canada who both loved and understood Jack. He now lived at Lakefield in Ontario and Jack hoped to meet him when they reached the state capital, Toronto.

Douglas had played an important part in Jack's war and its curious aftermath. In 1914, Jack had emerged from the Barrens determined to enlist in the Canadian forces as a private soldier. He had stayed at Lakefield while Douglas tried in vain to persuade him to take a commission in the Imperial Army, but Jack did not wish or feel able to lead men at this stage. So Private 2064 Hornby went to Europe and was among the Canadian Cavalry Division thrown in to defend the Ypres salient where, on 22 April 1915, they were subjected to the first use of poison gas in warfare. He survived four separate chlorine gas attacks at Ypres.

By September 1915, Hornby had overcome his scruples and had taken George Douglas's advice by applying for a commission with the South Lancashire Regiment. As he wrote to Douglas:

I think I deserve one, for I have given up a lot to join the army as you know and I am too old and have lived

too long with what one calls here the uncivilized races
. . . to ever get accustomed to the continual wrangling
and utter selfishness of the white races.

Gazetted Second Lieutenant, Jack is mentioned variously as
patrol officer (by his mother), sniping officer (by his Edmonton friend Yardley Weaver) and intelligence officer (by
Critchell-Bullock); his particular duties probably embraced
something of all three. Jack would have learned how to
conduct a night patrol whilst serving in the line at Ypres,
where the Canadians were known for their daring and inno-
vative raids across No Man's Land. The risks were considerable and Jack did not expect to survive long, but at least
there was initiative and resourcefulness in the job. He would
not, in the poet Wilfred Owen's phrase, 'die as cattle'.

With his extraordinary stamina, agility and resourcefulness, as well as his experience with the fearless Canadians,
Jack must have been a considerable asset in military oper-
ations of this kind. Despite the clear disillusionment he
expressed in his letters, at some point in spring or early
summer he did something conspicuously brave for which
he received the Military Cross, gazetted on 3 June 1916.
Frustratingly, no citation detailing his actions has been found
in military records, but they must have related to reconnaissance or raiding activity in the period before the Somme
offensive of July 1916 – possibly the elimination of a machine-
gun post or the retrieval of wounded comrades from a patrol.

It was during the Battle of the Somme itself, near the
Ovillers–La Boiselle front, that Jack was hit in the shoulder,
close to the neck, and possibly also in the middle of his back.

After a few days at a dressing station, then a field hospital, he was judged to have a 'blighty wound' and returned to England.

Jack was deeply traumatized. Apart from a brief period of officer training the previous autumn, he had spent almost two years in France, continually at or near the front. Now, as his wounds healed, his only thought was to get right away from Europe and back to the Barren Ground. So he walked out of the convalescence hospital near London and took ship to Halifax. He was Absent Without Leave: technically, a deserter.

After landing in Canada, he went to ground in a remote part of British Columbia. There followed several months of uncertainty, during which his friends tried to get him invalided out of the army with his infringement of King's Regulations wiped from the record. Even when these efforts finally succeeded, Jack was miserable and destitute. He longed for the Barrens, but his mother, angry at his desertion, had temporarily withdrawn financial support. Had it not been for a timely advance of $100 from George Douglas, he might not have returned to the North at all. Whether or not Jack ever repaid Douglas's loan, he never lost a sense of moral indebtedness to his friend.

But arriving now in Toronto with Edgar, Jack was disappointed to find Douglas away on business in New York — coincidentally renewing acquaintance with James Critchell-Bullock, who was trying to set up a lecture tour based on his Barren Ground wildlife films. Jack was able, however, to contact Douglas's wife, Kay, who had been staying with her father in the city. The two went to meet Jack and Edgar's train, and they all spent the next few hours together in downtown Toronto.

Perhaps because Kay Douglas, seeing Edgar's youth and naïvety, was the next to express concern about the Barrens, Jack now began talking very differently about his plans. He said he was thinking of going to Red Lake country, meaning the area in the extreme west of Ontario, about two hundred miles north-east of Winnipeg, to follow a gold rush there. Reinforcing the point, he had Edgar show their rail tickets, which were indeed for Winnipeg. This was a city no one aiming for the Barrens would need to stop at, while it was certainly the starting point for Red Lake. Recounting this story in a letter years later, George Douglas absolves Jack from a charge of lying. 'This was not from any intention to deceive, but his mind was like that – full of alternatives that he might choose from.' Nevertheless, there is no doubt that the Red Lake story was a complete red herring.

As they waved the train out of Toronto, Kay Douglas and her father did not themselves quite believe in Red Lake, and these misgivings stayed with them over the next few days. They even considered alerting the Royal Canadian Mounted Police. But what would they say? Jack had been so imprecise about his intentions that any information they could provide would be too vague to lead to meaningful action. In the end, nothing was done.

As the train steamed westward, skirting the coasts of Lake Huron and Lake Superior, Edgar found himself moved by the immensity of the country, especially the forests, and the great size of the lumber camps glimpsed at the trackside.

My word it was an Eye opener to me which just shewed how many thousands of square miles of dense forests and woodlands Canada still has where the woodsmans axe has never touched.

We passed the same sort of country all the morning and all the afternoon until about seven in the Evening when we Sighted Lake Superior for the first time. The Rail track does not keep close to the Lake but has to go a very zig-zag Course a little inland and steadily climbing all the time.

I thought I would not like travelling in the train when there is a sheer drop below but it Really was nice, in the Evening with the track Looping right down into the trees with Little streamlets and rivers flowing in between the rocks, while the train was going steadily up hill round bends where you could see the whole train with the engine coaling up all the time and vomiting clouds of smoke, it was magnificent in itself just as one sees advertised of a C.P.R. train in the Rockies.

At Jackfish Halt, on the evening of 6 May, they dined on grilled Lake Superior trout, which delighted Edgar. He was even more pleased when Jack told him this was 'what he gets when out in the bush'.

If the thirty-six-hour train journey from Toronto had been an eye-opener for Edgar, there was an even bigger one in Winnipeg, where Edgar discovered that his cousin was calling primarily to meet an unmarried twenty-eight-year-old Englishwoman called Olwen Newell, whom he had known for three years. They had met in Edmonton, following Jack's emergence from his second desperate solo winter near Fort Reliance. He had been making a few dollars as a guide to tourists hunting wild sheep in the Rockies. Olwen was living at the YWCA and working as a journalist, or perhaps a sub-editor, on the *Edmonton Gazette*. This paper had often been at the fore in promoting the Hornby myth, but Olwen was also personally interested in the Barren Lands. She had an ambition to do some kind of missionary or teaching work amongst the Indians.

Jack initially hoped that the well-educated Olwen would ghost-write his book *In the Land of Feast and Famine*. But by this time he had already met James Critchell-Bullock and, as the proposal for a serious journey into the Barrens developed, Olwen's role evolved into that of a largely unpaid secretary at the 'expedition office' which Critchell-Bullock and Hornby had set up to reflect their scientific pretensions and 'official' status. At some point in that winter of 1923–4, an attachment between Jack and Olwen developed, but, like everything connected with Jack, it was by no means straightforward.

Before 1914, Jack had not been particularly discreet about his sex life. At Dease Bay he had scandalized the missionaries with his liaison with Arimo, and at some point he contracted syphilis, which was cured by military doctors on his way to the war in 1914. During the 1920s, he had a number of more respectable lady friends – a widow in Montreal and, possibly, someone in the United States, where Jack had paid visits for the purpose of 'fund-raising'. She may be the person mentioned by Critchell-Bullock:

There was an American lady who wrote to him from Washington every Christmas and who he thought might be in the marriage market. He explained [to me] however that love was a thing of the past, and that in any case he 'had not the gall' to ask any woman to marry him.

Olwen was an attractive, intelligent young woman whose interest in Jack, with his piercing blue eyes, weathered face and easy, athletic way of moving, seems natural. He was also drawn to her and soon there were rumours of their engagement. A serious rift with Critchell-Bullock threatened when the Captain came back from a holiday in Vancouver and got wind of this. He immediately lost his temper and, thinking that she was trying to destroy the expedition, dismissed Olwen from her job. Jack, who was on his way to England for a short visit at the time, nearly abandoned the voyage in order to go back and beat up Critchell-Bullock. At the same time he hotly denied any engagement.

On quieter reflection it came down to a straight choice between Olwen and Critchell-Bullock: marriage, or another trip into the Barrens. He chose Critchell-Bullock. Before continuing on to England, Jack wrote to his lawyer and friend in Edmonton, Yardley Weaver, instructing him to make sure that Olwen's debts were paid and that she had the means, if she wished, to go to Winnipeg, where her brother was living. He had not seen her since.

But now, in 1926, he was still troubled by the sense that Olwen had been treated shabbily. He had always prided himself on his chivalry and so, after he and Edgar had settled into the Royal Alexandra Hotel, he set out to resolve his lingering scruples in an astonishing way. He made her an offer of marriage.

Olwen was greatly surprised by Jack's proposal and requested a little time to consider. Meanwhile, she saw a good deal of Edgar but very little of Jack, who was apparently frantically busy making arrangements for the expedition – telegraphing, holding meetings, making lists. In fact, there could be no serious start on the outfit for the Barrens until they reached Edmonton and this atypical activity looks like displacement, a cover for Jack's agitation and suspense.

In the end, Olwen formally refused Jack's proposal. To minimize the blow, she explained that there was no possibility of her marrying, as she would be going back to England as soon as she could afford the fare. Jack begged her to return to England, if she must, and 'wait for him'. He would continue with his expedition but promised to make sure she had enough money. What was more, he said, he was going to Weaver's office to redraft his will, leaving his entire fortune to her.

But Olwen would not change her mind and Jack, in another sudden flux of chivalry, went immediately to the Canadian Pacific Company and bought her a first-class ticket back to England. He also cabled her parents to tell them their daughter was coming home. Whether welcome or not, it was his last act of expiation. He does not appear to have altered his will.

In a sentimental coda to all this, it seems that Jack asked Olwen to kiss him good-bye at Winnipeg station, as the train prepared to depart. She offered only a peck on the cheek, at which he muttered, 'That is all I mean to you?' Lost for words, she squeezed his hand. Jack then asked her, again, to wait for him in England.

Did Edgar witness this? Although Jack behaved very differently in Winnipeg from the man who had earlier been so assured, Edgar's letters do not show that he was aware of Jack's sentimental predicament. Perhaps, in a place where everything was new and strange, Edgar had been too busy looking around him.

> Winnipeg, a City which I suppose has sprung up very quickly with no other for miles on any side, has very wide streets indeed and the traffic has got ample room everywhere. One thing that Looks nice here is the Horse drawn Vehicles. They are extremely smart and in pairs which always match ... Well kept and neat harness on them I must say they Look nice. I suppose grain is very cheap here, because even Cab horses get a whole bag of plain Oats for the 12 o' clock snack, without any Chaff thrown in to stop them bolting it.

But, most especially, Edgar was looking at Olwen, for this time he was assuredly smitten. During their visits to the shops downtown he continually wanted to buy her presents – a pearl necklace, a watch, a pen – all of which she tactfully refused.

In these few days Olwen had become very attached to Edgar, if only in a big-sisterly way. She had also begun to fear for him. The more she thought about it, the more doubtful she was of his going into the Barrens, and she told

Jack so. In a letter which Olwen later wrote to Edgar's mother, she gave a delicately skewed version of these discussions, editing out her own role:

> As Jack was very busy while in the city, I saw quite a lot of your son. He looked very well, and was in excellent spirits, but J. H. tried his utmost to dissuade him from going any further than Athabaska, telling him he could go back to the old country with some wild buffalo Jack was going to have sent to the Edinburgh Zoological Gardens. The morning they left Winnipeg, I had coffee with them at the station, and they were still arguing about how far Edgar was to go.

Nothing more is known of the mysterious zoo project. Possibly it was a spur-of-the-moment fantasy which Olwen, out of tact or loyalty to Jack, brought forward as a serious idea, to show him as a man struggling to do the right thing. She was also concerned to underline Edgar's courage and determination to see things through and not let Jack down. But her statement that Jack was 'arguing about how far Edgar was to go' is questionable. Jack didn't need to argue with Edgar about this matter. It was in his power to modify the trip, or cancel it entirely, for any reason.

It was Olwen who was arguing that Edgar should not go beyond Athabaska. But her rejection of his marriage proposal had left Jack thinking only of the Barren Ground, the caribou and the Thelon. The buffalo and Edinburgh Zoo were not mentioned again.

5. Harold

The journey's next stage, the last by Canadian Pacific, brought Jack back to Edmonton for the first time since he'd set out on his trip with Critchell-Bullock in July 1924. As the place where his legend had first sprung up, the city was of some significance to him. It had long been a busy mustering-station for adventurers and misfits, amongst whom the young and diminutive Jack had hardly stood out at first. But his return from war in 1917, and the decision to re-enter the Barrens immediately and alone, suddenly lent him new status. An article appeared in the *Edmonton Bulletin*, published on 16 June 1917, which can be seen as the real beginning of the Hornby myth. It represented Jack's life, in quite the T. E. Lawrence tradition, as 'a story that only an adventurous Anglo-Saxon could live'. After sketching his appearance – 'a shock of unruly brown hair unrestrained by a hat, a pair of mild blue eyes, looking out from a face still wrinkled with the pain it had lately borne' – the piece told how he had left his beloved Barren Lands to rally to the colours. Now he was back, a decorated hero, but a man obviously wounded in his spirit as much as his body. The article ended with a series of almost Arthurian flourishes:

Then he shoved out into the stream and we watched him until he drifted from sight, his bare head almost hallowed [*sic*] as the setting sun shot its golden rays aslant the river's silver water. There are many others who came from the Empire's outer edges to fight the battles of King and Country, but no others will return a further distance to their old life and work than Lieut. Jack Hornsby [*sic*], the explorer of Great Bear Lake.

This, despite the misspelling of his name, was the birth of Hornby of the North, the Hermit of the Arctic. With Jack's active encouragement, the notion had slowly spread and now, as Edgar had been finding, the Hornby name was known all along the route of the Canadian Pacific Railway. The letter Edgar posted to his mother before leaving Winnipeg glows with the boy's happiness and his confidence in the leadership of this famous man:

When I get to Edmonton I shall be on a stepping-off point from civilized people but still I am happy to think of it as one of Jacks old friends told me in Montreal, 'that I was with one of Canadas best and anyone who is with J. Hornby can never go wrong'.

So far, Jack's plans, in public at least, had been deliberately amorphous. As this letter seems to indicate, they now acquired definition. He had brought Edgar to Canada to show him life away from civilization – in the Barrens. Others had tried to talk Jack out of it, but now his resolve had hardened. To send the boy back at Lake Athabaska would not do at all, for this was well below the tree-line and, in the relative terms that Jack always used, was swarming with people. Only a winter in the Barren Ground fitted Jack's essential requirements.

Yet he had mixed feelings still. In a letter to George Douglas, written *en route* from Winnipeg to Edmonton, he suddenly gave vent to the weariness and disgust which, since the war, had sometimes taken hold of him. After Olwen's rejection, he had been feeling disconsolate at the thought that his compulsion for the Barrens would always make marriage, home and progeny impossible for him.

> I was very sorry not to have seen you at Toronto and regret that you cannot go North this year. I am heartily sick of the North and I really wish I had never buried myself in the wilds.

Jack also knew that Kay Douglas must have reported to her husband on their meeting in Toronto and, in the present letter, was at pains to minimize the scope and ambitions of the journey, whilst suggesting that it had some real, if small, commercial or scientific purpose.

> In all probability, I shall only make a trip to bring out a few more samples and then perhaps may settle down, somewhere on Vancouver Island. Will write again, when I reach Edmonton. With best wishes to all. Yrs v sinc Jack Hornby. PS There is great talk of the oil in Alberta.

In the event, he did not write from Edmonton and these few lines scribbled on the train were the last from Jack that Douglas would receive.

*

On arrival at Edmonton, Jack went as usual to Onoway, about forty miles away, where his (and Edgar's) relations, the Armitsteads, farmed. Jack deposited Edgar at the farm while he got on with assembling their outfit. For the next two weeks Edgar rode horses, helped out with the farmwork and was charmed by his reception.

> I think Mr and Mrs Armitstead are real toppers and she is awfully nice and said I always had a home in Canada by going there.

Dropping one day into the general store at Onoway to buy provisions or equipment, Jack met a figure he had known in Edmonton during 1923 and 1924. Harold Adlard, from Dorking in Surrey, now aged twenty-seven, was working behind the counter of the shop. As soon as he saw Jack, Harold reminded him of a promise made two years earlier.

The Adlards were the proprietors of a 200-year-old English printing and publishing firm, the Bartholomew Press, and were well heeled. In October 1917, Harold had joined the Royal Naval Air Service from his school, Lancing College, as a Probationary Flying Officer. He was posted to flying school at Vendôme in France, where British and French flyers trained together. He posted around sixty hours' flying time before returning to Cranwell in Lincolnshire to put the finishing touches to his education as a combat pilot.

The transformation of a fledgling airman into a pilot with wings normally took twenty-four weeks, but Harold's progress was interrupted by a long spell in hospital. This was probably the result of a flying accident, as air training was still a highly dangerous activity with trainee pilots being killed at a rate of one every two days. There is some evidence that Harold continued to be affected by his injury, whatever it was, and in one photograph in Canada he leans on a stick. But this cannot have seriously affected his physical fitness for, at last, he was passed for active service. The date, 11 November 1918, was the very day on which the war ended.

Harold stayed on in the service only a few more months, being placed on the reserve or 'unemployed' list on 30 May 1919. What he did between demobilization and sailing for North America is conjectural. Most likely he tried to work in the family business. But, for someone who had flown biplanes, office routine was tame, and Harold would not have been the first young man to find it impossible to work for his father. R. E. Adlard was a dour teetotaller – he had recently become publisher of the *National Temperance Quarterly* – and it is easy to see how the Mess drinking habits Harold had acquired in the service could have become a trigger for family rows. Adlard family lore has it that R. E. Adlard eventually ordered his son out of the house for drunkenness.

Harold's move to Canada in 1923 may have been influenced by the many Canadian pilots he had met in the wartime air force, whose informal, robust manner made their distant homeland seem a place of hope and fresh air – a place were Harold could drink whiskey if he chose. He crossed the Atlantic with a shipment of other similarly inclined young men, most of whom were to try out farming. Moving westwards, Harold eventually came to the Armitsteads' place at

Onoway, where he had been introduced to Jack Hornby. He does not seem to have taken much to farming and was struggling to make a living, yet he did not consider giving up on Canada. Quite apart from the rift with his father, it was rumoured that an unhappy love affair back home still troubled him.

Harold had also known Critchell-Bullock, and can be found in the Captain's photograph album posing in a group with the rancher Rochfort. In Canadian police reports, Harold was eventually to be described as an 'insurance agent at some time', and this must be how he kept body and soul together after he moved back to Edmonton. But he cannot have found the salesman's life any more congenial than the farmer's because, late in 1923, he tried his utmost to attach himself to the Hornby/Critchell-Bullock expedition into the Barrens. Jack, feeling sorry for Harold, told him he would be welcome to come along if Critchell-Bullock agreed. But the Captain didn't rate him and vetoed the proposal on the ostensible grounds that Harold was semi-disabled. Later he would write:

> Adlard had wanted to come with us, and Hornby would have taken him, but for the fact that I put my foot down. He was a first-class lad, but only in civilization. The opinion of some people was that a crash he had with the RAF had affected him.

To salve the young man's disappointment, Jack had then made a vague undertaking to take Harold on a future Barren Ground trip. Now, in the Onoway General Store, Harold was eagerly reminding Jack of the two-year-old promise, and assuring him he was ready to join the expedition that very day. Not quite so eagerly, Jack accepted him.

He took Harold on, as Edgar wrote in his next letter to Bron Dirion:

> as a kindness because the wolf was at the door, and would give him just what he thought fit at the end of the trip and deduct the extra expense for outfitting.

In reality there was more to it than this. It is true that one of Jack's most endearing qualities was his generosity, which could always, as in the case of Blanchet's fish on the Great Slave Lake in 1922, shade into the absurd. Jack gave away his food and clothing to the Indians, if he could. And his impulsive gift of a steamer ticket to England for Olwen had not been the first of its kind. In 1923, Cowper Rochfort, at whose ranch Jack had sometimes stayed, became 'bushed' and was behaving with sadistic cruelty towards his family. Jack intervened to rescue the victims, finding Mrs Rochfort a safe refuge in Edmonton and buying tickets home for herself and the children. In Critchell-Bullock's lurid account, when the vengeful husband came looking for his family, he threatened Jack with a revolver.

> Hornby rose from the easy chair in which he had been lounging, advanced on the rancher like a terrier on a mastiff and, calmly brushing the weapon aside, rapped out: 'Any more trouble from you, Rochfort, and I will thrash you within an inch of your life. I never fail to

keep my word, and you know it. Now go, before I set about you, you swine!' The man went.

So there is no doubting Jack's capacity for unexpected altruistic gestures. But he may also have felt that Harold's request was fortuitous. On a reckoning which he and Critchell-Bullock worked out when in tandem in the Barrens, three was really the minimum number for a safe expedition. This was the view Critchell-Bullock put forward in his official report.

A large party can afford to take greater chances than a small one, the loss of one individual where several are concerned need not necessarily be a serious matter. Even frostbite does not seem so awesome when it is known that skilled treatment will be received on reaching camp. But where only two men are concerned, and when the success of the expedition depends on the ability of those two men to remain fit, the whole aspect receives a different light.

Perhaps Jack was, after all, now taking notice of the warnings of Blanchet, Kay Douglas, Professor Mackenzie, Olwen Newell and others. By adding a third man to the party he could claim that he was further minimizing any risk.

When they moved back to Edmonton, just prior to departure on the northbound train, they put up at the Corona Hotel, run by Hornby's friend Bill Adamson. Olwen had sent a wire there to wish them well and, pointedly, it was not Jack, but Edgar who replied by letter.

Dear Miss Newell, I am writing this for Jack as he is
very busy getting fixed up to go north straight away.
We were away and did not get the wire until last night
and replied by wire this morning. Here's wishing good
trip and safe arrival.

At this point came Edgar's second meeting with Guy
Blanchet, who had arrived in the city ready to mount his
ambitious sortie towards Lake Athabaska, the Dubawnt River
and the water-threaded country between.

It was a purely social occasion and Jack was in confident
form, handing out copies of an old photograph of himself to
anybody who would accept one. The picture had been taken
in the early summer of 1919, and showed the explorer relaxing
on the ground in front of a roughly built log cabin. He
is studying a thick volume, apparently the Hudson's Bay
Company catalogue, which offered for sale rifles, ammunition, traps, canoes, clothing and all the necessaries of a life
in the North. Jack particularly liked this snapshot. It shows
him as he wanted to look in the eyes of the world: rugged
and weathered, his beard dark, hair unkempt and his clothing,
as usual, incongruent – denim trousers, a waistcoat, shirt and
tie and, on his feet, moccasins. The angle from which it is
taken and the seated posture suggest a man of greater stature
than he could claim in the flesh.

On parting, he and Blanchet said they might see each
other further up the trail. Then Jack, Edgar and Harold
launched into a sequence of final preparations. Edgar had
some last-minute purchases to make. He remembered his
father's advice to 'try to keep a diary' and he now dropped

into the shop of A. H. Esch, Commercial Stationers of Edmonton, and bought three large leather-bound notebooks, each with two hundred pages and the title *Records* impressed in gold letters on its cover. He also bought two printed books. The first was a volume of verse by Robert Service, *Songs of a Sourdough*, which purported to be 'a portrait written by an Indian girl of life in the North'. This he sent to his mother. The second was for himself, P. A. Taverner's *Birds of Eastern Canada*, published by the Canadian Department of Mines (Geological Survey) just four years earlier. Finally he picked out a small grey-covered Canadian pocket diary for 1926. Edgar was ready.

As for Harold, one of the few fragments that survive of his letters home shows the extent to which he, too, had bought into the Hornby legend.

> You remember I told you about a man named Hornby, the son of a famous cricketer, an explorer, prospector and trapper, the best known in the North today. His favourite pastime is rushing around the Barren Lands up in the Hudson Bay [area] and going where no white men have ever been before. Hornby suggested that I should accompany himself and his young cousin, just out from home, on this trip – duration two years, possibly.

Harold and Edgar arrived at the station with their baggage and outfit on 24 May, after Hornby had tipped off the Edmonton newspapers about his imminent departure. They had almost missed the weekly train for Waterways, the

67

northern railhead, and the departure was breathless. A photographer stood on the platform to capture the moment.

Their train, sarcastically referred to as the 'Muskeg Express', had opened for business in 1916 as a single-track railway three hundred miles in length. In its construction, unusual engineering problems had been posed by the dangerous stretches of marshy muskeg country along the route. In many places, to prevent the track buckling and sinking in the boggy ground, sections of rail were welded together to form continuous lines, which bent like a bow under the weight of the train. The train's speed was so pedestrian that in the summer it was said you could jump off the first car and pick a lard pail full of blueberries in the bush beside the track and still have time to catch the last car before it passed you by.

With 'the best accommodation on the train' secured, Jack, Edgar and Harold settled in for a sixteen-hour journey. Through the window, Edgar watched the apparently endless succession of poplar and spruce forests trundle by, interspersed by wide stretches of muskeg prairie. Using Taverner, he tried to identify the birds he saw: the spruce partridge, known as the fool hen for its trusting nature; the impertinent whisky-jack; the red-winged or soldier blackbird with its o-kee-ree cry; a heron poised statuesque beside a waterhole or, in the dusk, a hawk owl perching on top of a lightning-blasted tree trunk. Sometimes moose could be seen stalking through the trees and, from time to time, he would see a beaver dam thrown across a stream.

At some point during the long northern evening, there was a half-hour halt at Lac La Biche. Edgar wandered down to stretch his legs on the banks of the lake, where an old Indian was fishing with a stick and string with a trowl on the end and he caught one every two or three minutes which just showed how easy it is to live off fish which is far away from greedy inhabitants. These fish he caught were only Jackfish but they weighed several pounds.

With Lac La Biche behind them, they had crossed an important frontier. This was the furthest north for farming. There would now be no more Bible-conscious settlers, draining the marshes and breaking the stony land. Instead there were Swedish trappers, Syrian fur-traders, Scottish game-hunters – adaptable men who followed the pelts and the meat into the wilderness and came out when it suited them. On the train, Edgar was able to study several of the type – weathered, bearded, wide-hatted and dressed in a strange composite of European and Indian garb. Some travelled with women and children, which showed that family life could trickle into even the most unpromising places – even into the North.

Early in the morning, the three Englishmen were woken by a 'commotion'. One of the children on board had gone missing, and

after a search the train stopped and Some gangmen on the Line went back on a hand trolley and found the Little boy walking along following the track. He had fallen off the step when the train was going fast 18 MPH!! and had not hurt himself at all.

The Muskeg Express pulled into Waterways at ten in the morning. Although still well short of the Barren Ground, they had come as far as they could by familiar modes of travel. From now on progress could only be made by water routes – of which there were plenty – or cross-country travel. In either case, the only motors they could count on would be their own bodies, fuelled by whatever food they could hunt, fish or carry.

6. Canoe

The Muskeg Express, precarious though it was, had made Waterways a bottleneck through which almost all traffic passed into a 2,500-mile system of navigable rivers and lakes between here and the Arctic Ocean. The railhead was the best possible means of access to the lands around the Great Bear, Great Slave and Athabaska lakes, so that a motley collection of individuals funnelled through it. Hudson's Bay Company men, surveyors, trappers and their outfits, traders, prospectors, missionaries, Royal Canadian Mounted Police, Indians, half-breeds, sportsmen and adventurers – all came in and out of the North through the Waterways railhead and its neighbouring riverside settlement, Fort McMurray.

Edgar was captivated by that rich, promiscuous cross-section of northern life, but Jack could not refrain from passing disparaging remarks. He enjoyed the company of other travellers and swapped anecdotes endlessly with them. But he also felt uneasy. He had first visited McMurray in 1908 with Cosmo Melvill, when it was a tiny outpost of no particular significance. Now it already had a couple of churches and hotels, the odd rattletrap motor vehicle running up and down the main (but still only) street, a man-made road to the station three miles away, and several stores and trading establishments. There were even European women to be seen in town – the resident wives and daughters of men such as the Lutheran pastor and the Hudson's Bay Company factor, as well as up-country women coming in to provision the cabins in which they and their families struggled to survive by hunting and trapping along the Athabaska River.

All this painfully reinforced Jack's entirely subjective sense that his country was becoming overrun. The 1921 population census had counted less than 8,000 individuals in the whole of the vast North-Western Territories, of which a minority were European. Fort McMurray was at that time too small to have its population (of less than 250) separately itemized, and was mostly of Indian or mixed race. But Jack's eyes persisted in seeing overpopulation wherever he looked – and interlopers, travelling in obscene comfort from the South. His old preference for unplanned and self-sufficient travel had hardened in his mind from a habit into a law. No one, he thought, should go into the Barren Ground unprepared for the bitterest hardship – a monastic principle of self-denial and asceticism that was being fatally undermined by every rail line, motor road, police post and motorized canoe that penetrated into the North. A few months earlier, when composing his caribou and musk-ox report, he had given voice to this pessimism.

The day of hardship & exploration in the Arctic Regions is now a thing of the past. One can realize with what difficulties & hardships travellers used to be beset. Now the routes are mapped, transportation is easy & instead of months it is now only a question of days. Previously it was the Explorer, now it will be the Tourist who traverses these regions.

Arriving in the busy community of McMurray, he came face to face with this reality. The old freemasonry of a (very) few hardened men, who felt about the North as a secret society feels about its rituals and oaths, had become diluted into meaninglessness. From this perspective Jack, the Hermit of the North, was a dinosaur, destined for extinction as his habitat was despoiled. But there was a more bitter truth even than this. He too, in his own essence, was being bitterly compromised. Once he would have canoed right past Mc-Murray, after joining the Athabaska River 50 miles upstream at Athabaska Landing and shooting a succession of dramatic rapids along the way. Now his use of the Muskeg Express made him part of the betrayal.

Overcompensation for inner guilt made Jack ever more extreme in his condemnation of cushy travel. Critchell-Bullock wrote of Jack's 'hook-or-crook' method of travel:

> There were many more things of which Hornby disapproved than approved, and from among the former he reserved his most scathing comments for government-sponsored trips and expeditions. He called them 'so many damned police patrols' . . . 'What do these men know of travelling,' he would ask, 'when they go off equipped and backed by all the resources of the State? There is not one of them who could stay with me if it became a matter of living off the country. They are not accustomed to hardship and it is foolish to call them travellers.'

No argument could persuade Hornby that any Arctic,

or sub-Arctic exploit was worthy of commendation unless the principals had gone out on a shoestring, and returned by the skin of their teeth.

It was this mind-set which made Jack so difficult to deflect from his ultimate objective of entering the remotest part of the Barren Ground. But he does seem to have taken notice of the concerns expressed by men like Blanchet about his equipment, and he responded by assembling what looks like a relatively competent outfit.

Apart from the canoe itself, the heaviest piece of equipment was a McClary's free-standing patent BC camp stove of thick sheet metal. A heavy hinged door, with a sliding draught-check, gave access to the firebox. At the rear was a thick, detachable back-plate and into this fitted one end of an angled stove-pipe which connected, at the other end, to a chimney-pipe. Other bulky items to be transported to the Thelon included the chimney-pipe itself, a canvas tent and groundsheet, red Hudson Bay blankets, mattresses, pack sacks, fishing nets and other tackle, a collection of cups, tins, pots, pans, plates and cutlery, a Primus Stove, a hand-cranked Swedish meat-grinder fitted with a fixing clamp, a felling axe and light tripping axe, other tools such as file, hammers, drill and nails, several sets of traps, two cabin trunks containing technical equipment including binoculars, a compensated aneroid barometer, a Kodak camera and photographic and specimen-collecting gear. Then, at some point, three sheets of window glass were added to the load.

There were three rifles, the weapons upon which the trio were to depend for much of their food. These were of .303

calibre: a 25–35 Savage, a BSA and the Lee Enfield Mark 2, the last of which was a variation of the standard British infantry rifle in the Great War. There was, significantly and perhaps fatally, no shotgun.

Each of the three men also had a bulky leather suitcase containing clothes, books, writing materials and other personal effects. Their clothing, most of it derived from sheep's wool, was just the sort of garb usually worn in cold climates by adventurous Englishmen: canvas or woollen trousers, woollen underwear and knitted sweaters, flannel shirts and tweed jackets. To warm their necks they packed silk scarves or cravats and their preferred footwear, until they acquired moccasins, consisted of thick woollen socks inside nailed boots. Military-style puttees bound their ankles. Apart from moccasins, the only item of indigenous clothing they carried into the Barrens was one native-style, caribou-skin parka to be shared between the three of them. This was the single most practical and weatherproof item in the inventory and it is very surprising they were not equipped with one each.

In an attempt to cut down on weight and bulk, Jack had insisted that Edgar leave behind much of his superfluous luggage, amongst which he included the Prayer Book and Bible which Marguerite Christian had given him. Jack does not seem to have thought it contradictory that he himself retained, in the bottom of his own suitcase, an evening suit, black tie, dress shirt and set of gold shirt studs. He had also packed a pair of hairbrushes carrying his own monogram mounted in silver, and two silver-capped bottles for Eau de Cologne or Macassar oil.

This is approximately the extent of the durable items that

were to be carried into the Barrens. They cannot have weighed much less than a ton and the consumable stores remained to be added. It is more difficult to estimate the quantity of these. There were tin cases of 25–35 Winchester and British .303 ammunition, two thousand rounds in all, says Edgar in one of his letters. There were boxes of eight-inch black wax candles and jerry-cans filled with spirit-fuel for the primus. In a medicine chest there were bandages, lint, iodine, aspirins, brandy and a bottle of eyewash, with a special eyewashing-cup shaped like a wine glass, as a precaution in case of frozen-eye or snow-blindness.

Of food, there was pemmican, flour, oats and sugar in cotton sacks, and hardtack biscuits. There was certainly a good quantity of Tuckett's Virginia tea – a camp-site staple for Jack – packed in a red tin box with a hinged lid. The box has survived and is now in the Museum of the North at Yellowknife, with a number of other items from Jack's outfit. The empty cork-stopped Bovril jar is one of very few exhibits giving evidence of extra luxuries packed. But at the start there was a few days' supply of bacon, jam and perhaps dried fruit.

This, then, was Jack's outfit. It was paid for, presumably, out of his personal capital or with help from his ever-reluctant mother, and only by his own austere, hook-or-crook stand-ards could it be described as luxurious – no sleeping bags were packed, for instance. Yet it must be said that he had provided the basis in hardware for a reasonably comfortable three-man camp. It is impossible to quantify the food that was packed, but it should be noted that to some who saw the food supplies *en route*, they looked seriously deficient.

So the hardware was extensive, if not completely adequate, while the consumables were kept to a bare minimum, sacrificed to Jack's bullish confidence in his ability as a hunter. The outfit is therefore the clearest expression of Jack's inner conflict at this time: on the one hand was his recognition that Edgar and Harold needed protection; on the other was his belief in simple hardship on the trail. Jack could not rid himself of the depressive sense that the North as he once knew it was being spoiled by intruders and regulation. Already it was necessary to hold a Resident Hunting and Trapping License and, somewhere along the route, Jack had obediently acquired one. But he knew that the next generation of travellers would be all too easily seduced into the new labour-saving travel, and he wanted to make two individuals, at least, aware of how things ought to be done. For Edgar and Harold, therefore, there was an element of initiation about all this. Jack wanted to make them witnesses to the true path.

At Waterways, the canoe and outfit were laboriously hauled from the train to the river, and the 'Chestnut' canoe, bought at Edmonton, was launched and loaded. Except for any portages, this would be their conveyance for the rest of the trip. It was a sizeable cedarwood vessel, twenty foot long and square-sterned to accommodate the recent innovation of an outboard motor. George Douglas had been a strong advocate of outboards since the development of the Johnson diesel-driven engine which, at two and a half horsepower, could comfortably drive a boat against a river's current or a head wind in lakewater. Needless to say, Jack did not have one, intending to use paddle power only, except when conditions might enable him to set a sail.

Much of the first part of the journey – about four hundred miles – could in fact have been completed by one or other of the paddle steamers which plied these great waterways: up the Athabaska River to Fort Chipewyan at the tip of the Athabaska Lake, across the lake to the Slave River and thence downstream to Smith Landing, Fort Smith and Fort Resolution on the southern shore of Great Slave Lake. If they had done this they would have left the steamer at Resolution. Its orders took it down the Mackenzie River to Aklavik and the Beaufort Sea, while Jack was heading to the east end of Great Slave Lake itself. But this is all academic. Jack and his two companions intended to canoe the entire distance.

But in the event it was four travellers, not three, who pushed the canoe off from the riverbank at Fort McMurray on Friday 28 May. The party had been joined by a man from the train, identified in Edgar's letters only by the initials J.M. He was a late straggler of Blanchet's surveying party, hurrying north to join up with the others at Fort Chipewyan, and Jack must have been pleased to give him a lift. As an experienced traveller (Blanchet would not have hired a novice), J.M. provided a second experienced paddle for the first leg of the voyage, while Harold and Edgar learned canoemanship.

For Edgar, the adventure he had dreamed of back in England was now beginning. He was impatient to record his experience of camp life and did so in his first diary entry, not in one of the books he had bought for the purpose, but in a notebook of Jack's containing the caribou report of 1925 in manuscript and a few jottings for *In the Land of Feast and Famine*. Perhaps Esch & Co.'s notebooks were inaccessibly packed and he had pulled out the first volume he could reach.

His excitement is apparent from the breathless tone of these first diary words, which may have been written at around midday.

28th May 1926. McMurray. I woke up to hear Jack Lighting the fire at 3.30 a.m. and soon J.M. and Harold woke up after inquiries as to where the bacon was. Found bacon and cooked breakfast and then started to clean up the Camp and unpack the Canoe. At 7 a.m. after buying a little extra food we started down the Athabasca. A moderately strong headwind was against us after an hour or so and hopes of making time were bad.

11 o'clock we pulled in to have a spell and some Lunch. Jack and J.M. hunt for insects while Harold cooks a meal of Eggs and bacon and I sit in the smudge, funking the mosquitoes.

12 o' clock we push off again with wind still blowing against us.

This was an isolated journal entry, however. Edgar must have decided to put his energy for the time being into letters home, at least for as long as these could be posted, proceeding over the next month to treat his parents to an entertaining account of each stage of the long journey to Fort Reliance.

In all, he wrote three long journal-letters – one sent to his mother from Fort Smith, a second to his father from Fort Resolution, and a third, never posted, telling of events as far as Reliance.

The Athabaska River, down which Edgar was now so enthusiastically paddling, is one of the world's great rivers. Comparable in scale to the Danube, it rises from the Athabaska Glacier in the Rocky Mountains and flows through a succession of deep valleys and ravines on its way north-east to Lake Athabaska.

'The Athabaska is a fine big river,' wrote Edgar, 'with towering tar sand banks thickly wooded with spruce and poplar.' Until a few weeks earlier the stream had been thickly frozen, but now the air was warm, the ice had cleared and the brown water moved in a stately flow. By the end of their hard first day, despite pulling the paddle through choppy water against the wind, Edgar's mood had not changed and he continued his next journal-letter, finding words that effectively convey a hard day's work completed by the blissful contentment of camp.

> We paddled on till 5 o' clock and then pitched camp on an island after doing 35 miles. After supper I curled up in a Hudson Bay blanket and fell off to sleep under canvas on our little island home with the ducks and night owls flying round and feeding at the water's edge within a few yards of us.
>
> On Saturday we started at 6.45 having finished the Eggs and jam knowing our next meal would not be white mans grub but Pemican.

At the next camping place they were held up by the strengthening wind followed by rain. Edgar woke in the night and heard Jack moving around outside, covering the stores and upturning the canoe to keep it dry. The next day Jack decided they would rest all day and travel by night – a magical experience which again drew an evocative response from Edgar.

Travelling by night is very nice when there are no mosquitos and it is just a.1. with us. Not a breath of wind, the Moon was out bright and the Stars bright above amongst the northern Lights. In front of us we could just see a limited space of the river with a glassy moonshine gradually disappearing into the darkness. All around the duck were alighting and flying off and the owls and night hawks flying around.

Two nights later they were at Fort Chipewyan.

Chipewyan, named after the Chipewyan Indians inhabiting the region, was an old Hudson's Bay Company depot and staging post on the way north. Sir John Franklin had been here in 1821 on his first attempt to locate the north-west passage by trekking to the polar sea from the middle of continental North America – the boot-eating exploit which made his name. A hundred years later, the post had adapted to modern conditions, with a large HBC store, accommodation for travellers, independent fur-trading stations run by Syrians and even a Chinese restaurant.

At this stage, whatever his thinking until now, Hornby's mind was definitely made up. Under questioning by the 'old pals' he met everywhere, he now spoke of a spot in the Barrens which he had explored with Critchell-Bullock the previous year. It was on a wooded bend of the Thelon River, an oasis of vegetation in the midst of the Barrens, yet hundreds of miles from the nearest settlement. This place could be reached from Reliance by water, albeit with some fierce portages along the way, and he was sure – absolutely sure – that there would be game aplenty: birds, fish and overwintering caribou. And he was just as sure of the fox fur they would find.

This was the plan he unfolded to Guy Blanchet when they met for the third and last time at Chipewyan. Edgar's letter mentions an encounter with an 'old pal' in the Hudson's Bay Store, but does not mention Blanchet. This is odd. Edgar had already told his parents about 'Mr Blanchette who is an old pal and whom he [Jack] introduced to grandma a few years ago in town' – the man with whom they had had a game of golf and a pleasant day canoeing on the Ottawa River. The 'pal' in the Hudson Bay Store is probably someone else, but it is significant that the Chipewyan meeting with Blanchet goes unmentioned in Edgar's narrative. It turned out to be an argumentative occasion.

Three accounts of the meeting were written by Blanchet many years later, and these are consistent with each other. In the first of these, he remembered urging Jack not to risk Edgar on the Thelon.

> We talked things over at C[hipewyan]. I offered to take both H. and Christian, not the other chap. H. was interested but said his plans were made and he wouldn't

change them. I warned him about no caribou on the
Thelon, from my own observation and what I had
heard from [the trappers] Blackie Boblett[s] and Souci
King.

But Jack was unimpressed, insisting that there would be
plenty of caribou, and also that he 'expected to make a
fortune in foxes for Christian'. Finally Jack asserted, as he
nearly always did when preparing to go north, that 'this was
to be his last trip'.

Three and a half years later, Blanchet was to remember
likewise that:

They arrived while I was at Chipewyan with Adelard
[*sic*]. I did my best to persuade him not to winter down
the Thelon and I did not like Adelard. I proposed that
I could take him and Edgar on the trip I was making
but he said he had made his plans and promised Edgar
and Adelard and would not change.

In Blanchet's memory, his concern arose not just from his
distrust of Harold, but because he did not believe that three
men could live self-sufficiently at the place Jack proposed.
Just as Jack was certain of the opposite, Blanchet was sure,
as he put it to Jack's biographer on yet another occasion:

that this was a summer breeding ground but not a
winter range, that there would be no fish in the Thelon
and that the caribou pass through in the autumn and
late spring only. He did not argue but put on his puckish

83

grin. He knew better. Christian resented any question of Jack's knowledge and ability.

Edgar must have been angered by Guy Blanchet's rejection of Harold, whom he now thought a 'nice chap', but even more so by the doubts cast on Jack's expertise. His cousin was, after all, the author of a recent special government report on the caribou and might be regarded as the most up-to-date authority on it. A growing dislike of Blanchet and his views may have been why the surveyor was blanked from the letters home. It was also at the root of Edgar's wilful, mischievous exaggeration of the hardships of the journey they had just completed from McMurray.

> Christian told me they had set out with a pound of tea, a box of matches and a fish net and had travelled day and night.

It is likely that Blanchet's views on caribou in the Thelon, whatever they were in 1926, became more definite in hindsight. If, when he first expressed them, he had been challenged on his certainty that caribou did not winter on the Thelon, he would have had to admit that no one knew the truth. It is also doubtful that he was able at that time to draw on conversations with Blackie Bobletts on the subject. This backwoodsman certainly knew the country well enough by 1929 to guide the police patrol sent to investigate events at the Hornby cabin. But he had not been down the Thelon before.

In a letter written much closer to the events, H. S. Wilson recounted:

When one reflects on the lack of positive knowledge regarding the distribution of game during the winter months, it is not difficult to understand ... Hornby, and probably others, thought that since the caribou migrate to the woods for the winter, they should be, during the winter, as abundant in the isolated woods along the Thelon River as they are at the edge of the main woods north-east of Great Slave Lake. Prior to Hornby's trip there was no definite information on this point, as heretofore no one had attempted to winter in such an oasis, separated from the main woods by many miles of Barren Lands.

On the other hand, Blanchet's doubts about a risky experiment on the Thelon with two greenhorns would have been fully endorsed by Wilson, who went on to write:

If therefore caribou do not winter in such a place but return to the edge of the main woods, it is evident that Hornby would have to rely upon other animals as a source of food. This would leave the party in a serious position, for, in addition to cutting down their food supply, they would be unable to obtain adequate winter clothing, without which it is almost impossible to imagine travel in the Barren Lands.

In 1926, then, the question was, were there caribou on the Thelon during winter? Nobody knew for sure. The title of Jack's proposed memoirs about the Barren Ground. *In the Land of Feast and Famine*, refers to the unpredictable movements of the region's predominant food source. At any given time, whether feast overcomes famine is a fifty-fifty bet, red or black. Jack's project was effectively staking his life, and that of his friends, on the toss of a coin.

7. Towards Resolution

On Wednesday 2 June, they left Guy Blanchet and his awkward questions behind them. He and five other men, including J.M., would pursue their mapping at the east end of Athabaska Lake and along the Dubawnt River, while Jack canoed into the Slave River, which drained the west end of the lake and flowed in a straight, purposeful line towards the North.

The canoe would have been lighter with only three in it, although Jack had filled some of the vacated space with additional supplies from the store at Chipewyan. Yet progress was easier and swifter than before. With the wind now blowing from the south, they rigged up a mast and the canvas groundsheet that doubled as a sail and sped along with the wind and the current.

The Slave is an enormous river, in parts over a mile wide. Some of its stretches follow a course for miles between wooded banks, as straight as a Roman road. The canoe hugged one bank or the other, sometimes rolling in swift eddying currents, sometimes pushing smoothly forward with startling speed through lazy, listless water. Trailing his hand overboard, Edgar observed the whiskered noses of the musk rats, lifted like periscopes above the surface, as the small aquatic rodents battled upstream in search of a secluded beach on which to squat and stuff their mouths with grass.

On pieces of blanched driftwood sat all manner of wild duck, watching their progress.

At midday, the sunlight glared from a cloudless sky. The heat ashore was intense, up to 100 degrees, and when this moderated in the evening, the mosquitoes came out. Rising in vengeful hunger from the surface of the water, they were especially delighted by Edgar.

> The mosquitoes were out rather bad and they played old nick with me because I am green and have got juicy blood for them. It was simply awful all the next day too I could not keep them off my feet although I had a blanket round my feet, they bit me somehow or other and I felt like jumping into the river to get out of the way.

Jack did not seem over-bothered by the biting and he told Edgar it was no use complaining. The menace would be with them all summer, getting worse as they went further north, where the pests roamed about 'in clouds'. Oil of citron could be spread on the skin as a repellant, but one's sweat washed it off almost at once and the mosquitoes returned. In the evenings, when they camped, they would light a bonfire of green brushwood upwind to create a 'smudge' that would envelop them in smoke. Although uncomfortable in itself, the smudge would help Edgar beat the mosquitoes until he developed some measure of immunity.

There was, however, no immunity from the blackfly, a fearsome daytime predator with a razor-edged gouge for a nose. Even Indians avoid places where this fly congregates in numbers, and it is the reason the moose can be seen patiently standing for hours in a lake, the water up past its dangling dewlap. The blackfly is also called the Bulldog fly and is quite simply a ravenous vampire. It takes out lumps of flesh and leaves poison behind to make a burning, swollen wound like a boil. Critchell-Bullock remembered that on one occasion, 'the blackflies attacked us so viciously that my beard was a mass of blood and to rub it was to paint my hand as with a brush of scarlet'. This insect's only positive quality is that it does not bite at night. Then it leaves the field to the mosquito.

After just two days of downstream sailing they reached the only portage in the five-hundred-mile journey between McMurray and the Great Slave Lake. This was at the small settlement of Fitzgerald, which had been previously known as Smith Landing. Between here and Fort Smith the river fans out around a series of island clusters. The flow becomes shallower and faster, accelerating for sixteen miles past jagged rocks and smooth loaf-like boulders. There are three distinct sets of rapids – the middle one known as Pelican Rapid after the fowl which nest, happy and unmolested, on one of the islands in the stream. The pelicans' complacency is understandable. These are highly dangerous waters and it is quite impossible for any large canoe or vessel to pass over them.

The only solution is a portage – the transport of vessels and their cargoes by land. For this purpose, horses and carts shuttled continually between Fitzgerald and Fort Smith, carrying canoes, scows, flat-bottomed York boats and travellers' outfits. But with other travellers ahead of him in the queue (providing further proof, if he needed it, of the increasing numbers coming north), Jack was impatient at the delay. As Edgar reported:

> The freight and stuff has to cross the Portage by wagon and teams to Fort Smith. Jack arranged to get our junk over and then saw some old friends and got Provisions at the Store and decided to walk to Smith in the night. I had a mosquitoe net for my head this time and we started walking at 2 o'clock (a.m. 4 June) along the wagon trail. The flies were bad but the air was Cool and I felt like a walk after canoeing for 300 miles.

The portage road followed an old Indian trail built on glacial silt, the surface a fine white dust four inches deep that puffed up underfoot like chalk powder – unless it had been raining, when it formed a clogging mud. It was on this road that Edgar, for the first time on the trip, had a taste of Jack's powerful, relentless walking style.

> Jack certainly is a walker and he said we could not walk fast as he is not the man he used to be and felt like taking Life more easily now, but he walked jolly fast in my opinion and I soon learnt that I didn't know how to Walk because we could go faster [still] as he showed at times. We got here in about 3¾ hours and I was darn tired and my Ankles were Like footballs and I could only just get my socks off. I bathed my feet and put on Zambuk after getting to the house of Jacks old Pal who has been here 40 years.

This hospitality and Zambuck ointment (familiarly known as 'Yellow Peril') to ease his insect bites came from Pete McCallum, whom Jack had known since 1908. McCallum was the fourth European on Cosmo Melvill's expedition to the north of Great Bear Lake, and he and Jack had become confidants. In origin a Scots carpenter, McCallum had a fund of tall stories about the North and life on the trail. Edgar listened enraptured as Old Pete told of times

> when he was about the only Person in Fort Smith and how he went to Edmonton by dog team, and also about being the only white man to take a dog team to Regina Show many years ago and how he was greeted and entertained by Lord Aberdeen the Governor-General. It was the best Conversation I have ever had with any man on the old days and he is now 72 years old and active as a cat and says he is going trapping this winter and will try and find Jack if he can.

Fort Smith was the administrative centre of the North Western Territories of Canada, with a hotel, a mission church, police barracks, a couple of restaurants and a few General Stores as well as a handful of private homes. Around the edge of town was a ring of Indian shacks and tepees, untidy semi-permanent camps acrid with woodsmoke and echoing to the ceaseless howling of starving dogs. The town had a reputation as a raffish place, the pioneer explorer Warburton Pike finding it 'the most disreputable establishment I had come across in the North'. Jack took part in Smith's rough, inebriated celebrations in May 1920 for the

250th anniversary of the Hudson's Bay Company. He played in a game of scratch football, hurling himself into the fray with such enthusiasm that he claimed to have suffered a broken leg. This did not prevent him from departing a few days later, all alone, for the North, with his leg 'in splints'.

It took two full days for the portage of the canoe and outfit to be completed, but Edgar, with his swollen insect-bitten ankles, was happy to stay resting and yarning with old Pete. He wrote a letter full of his happiness – about Jack, the experiences that lay immediately ahead and the future beyond:

> I dont expect to get a letter for 18 months at least unless plans are altered and I cant send out a letter from here onwards so please don't get worried about me because I am safe as a house with Jack . . . This is, although bad with flies, a wonderful life and one could not wish for better. After going this trip with Jack I shall never be in need of a job if I want one. I can be independent of any man because I can make my own headway in lots of ways.

But Jack chafed at the delay, knowing this was not like missing a train at Crewe. He was anxious to press on to Fort Reliance and to begin the slowest and most difficult stretch of the trip – 300 miles by water and portage to the Thelon oasis, his intended winter quarters. The equivalent journey with Critchell-Bullock had taken roughly three months and, with the Arctic summer ending in August, the freeze-up due any time after mid-September, and with no dogs in his outfit, it was important to be securely camped on the Barrens before the really cold weather set in.

It is hard to know what Harold thought. In the few fragments of a letter home that have survived, he is determined to be upbeat about the journey. He was particularly struck by the romantic side of the project – the entry into unexplored territories, the journey down a river where scarcely a dozen parties had gone before, living by their rifles in a cabin built with their own hands where they could 'watch the animals go by'. There is no hint here that technicalities of weather, or caribou migration patterns, exercised him at all.

On the third day of their stay at Fort Smith, 6 June, Edgar celebrated his eighteenth birthday. As if to mark the day, he dug out the grey Canadian pocket diary, turned to the page headed Personal Details and carefully pencilled in: *name*, Edgar Vernon Christian; *birth date*, 6 June; *age*, 18; *height*, 6 foot; *weight*, 11 stone 4 pounds. Rather oddly, he does not mention the birthday in the letter he wrote to his mother next day, the last he thought he would mail. It was still being scribbled up to the moment when 'the Ford Car which is taking this letter is due to start for Fitzgerald to catch the Post'.

> If I can get a letter out by any trader or trapper in the North I will but it will be brief in Comparison to the Long history and Life I shall be storing up on this trip.

In fact, Edgar managed an even longer despatch at their next stage, near Fort Resolution, and it is thanks to this, addressed to Colonel Christian, that we have a rather detailed account of the next two-day stage of the journey. At some point during 7 June, Jack was offered mechanized assistance to complete his passage down the Slave River. The RCMP corporal stationed at Smith was motoring down to Resolution to deliver a new boat to the police post there. He had some mission fathers as passengers, but told Jack he would also take his party, canoe and baggage. Concerned about time, Jack once again compromised on his principles and took the offer. They were up all night packing the outfit down to the Mountie's landing stage and at first light they set off, watched to vanishing point by old Pete McCallum.

George Douglas describes the Lower Slave, flowing now through a densely forested alluvial plain, as an uninteresting river to travel down. Its sandy banks become progressively lower and more featureless, and its great width makes it resemble a lake rather than a river. But Edgar was caught up in the excitement of travelling by motor boat for the first time.

We started from Smith at 3 a.m. and had all our outfit on board one boat which was Lashed alongside another bigger boat which was to be taken down to the Police stationed at Resolution. When it came to starting the Engine of the bigger boat wouldnt start so the small one was used while the Police man mended the other. Jack steered while I drove the Engine for [the] first hour. Then there was a Roar and more speed from the 20 h.p. Engine on the other boat so we shut off and left it to the big boat. The weather was bad and very windy but I was rather pleased because it kept the mosquitoes away. After Jack had been Steering for a couple of hours one of the Fathers volunteered to and he was a nice old chap joking away [about] getting wet and Cold while his pals were sitting inside Reading bibles and telling their beads at odd times. After breakfast Jack Let me have a time at steering and showed me how to tell whether there were likely to be sandbars by the formation of the banks and how to steer according to the wind and waves and current. At first it looked Easy but it keeps one on the Look out all the time for floating trees and Logs and depth of water.

They travelled all day and night and Edgar was on steering watch early next morning as they approached the delta of the river. Here the stream rayed out into numerous different channels, only one of which led to Fort Resolution, while the others gave directly on to Great Slave Lake itself.

This time I had to steer Expecting to come to a channel which would take us to Resolution without going on to Great Slave Lake. Somehow the Map was not Correct and I couldnt keep track of where we were Except that we were travelling due north by the Compass. By the map the river should have been straight but we zig-zagged for about 20 miles until I saw the Lake in front of us and then I knew something was wrong. I woke Jack up and he was just as puzzled as I was and Eventually it was decided not to go into the Lake because it was much too rough but go down the nearest

Channel and stop at an RC Mission Saw mill which was 10 miles from Resolution.

From the mill, Jack and the Mountie took the canoe back to Fort Resolution while Edgar and Harold rested and wrote letters. There were a few buildings – seven in the sketch map Edgar made of the area at the back of his diary – and these were surrounded by natives encamped for the summer on scattered sites among the trees a short distance removed from the river bank. Although they had made camp, they were apparently looked after by the family of Alex Loutitt, a Scottish-Cree trader, and his mixed-race wife, Helen. Mrs Loutitt fed them and she also made them moccasins. Harold and Edgar watched the procedure with an interest so keen that it struck the Loutitt daughter Mabel, to whom moccasin-making was second nature, as utterly stupid.

Like every traveller new to the North, the first thing that struck Edgar about such settlements as this was the howling of dogs – 'the meanest brutes out. Mostly 3 parts wolf'. In winter, these Indian dogs were an essential part of the hunting effort. If not harnessed in teams to pull sleds on which tepees, camp equipment, traps and killed meat were transported, they were loaded with large saddlebags made of moose or caribou hide. Typically, a single dog packed a load up to roughly 75 per cent of its own weight from thirty-five pounds, half that of a man, to as much as fifty pounds in the case of a big, well-fed animal.

In winter, at the peak of their condition, they could be beautiful, imposing creatures with large wolfish heads, muscled haunches and legs, outsize paws and luxuriant coats.

But in summer they were unemployed and kept on a fraction of their winter rations. Skinny, mangy, fly-bitten, ill-tempered and ravenous, they skulked around the camp, unable to satisfy themselves except in savage outbursts of fighting. The Indians' harshness towards these animals – not only starving them but, if they felt like it, savagely beating them – routinely provoked the outrage of visiting Europeans, who thought of dogs as companions and work-mates. To the Indian, a dog was a utility.

The native camps that Edgar saw beside the Great Slave Lake, whose air thrummed with tom-toms and was torn by the weird, screeching song that accompanied the Indians' long gambling sessions, provided a cross-section of all the tribes inhabiting both forested land and Barren Ground that lay to the north of Lake Athabaska as far as the Arctic Circle and the Mackenzie River. Summering in the Resolution area, these were remnants and stragglers of those who, each year on Treaty Day, travelled to the post to collect five dollars per person from the government, their entitlement in compensation for the white man's use of their land.

The culture of these Indians seemed startlingly improvident and casual to the visitor from civilization, though it enshrined a familiar division of labour. The men reserved to themselves all the hunting and dog mushing. The women – who were forbidden to touch any of the hunting, trapping or fishing gear, or even to paddle a canoe across the line of a fishnet – did the remaining work of child-rearing, food preparation, tailoring, collecting water and all matters pertaining to the camp.

The most important principle by which the Indians lived was communal sharing. As nomads they made no attempt to

97

save or accumulate goods, moving camp swiftly every few weeks and putting down wherever they felt like ending a particular movement. When meat was available, it was distributed equally, with only the back fat and the tongue reserved exclusively for the man who had killed. The effect was a kind of social levelling: the best hunters being forced to subsidize the idle and incompetent.

To an eye like Edgar's it must have seemed an incurably primitive way of life. Jack had many stories of the natives' unaccountable superstitions, older and more durable than the superficial Catholicism most had adopted. The women were forbidden to cross the path of a man whilst menstruating. No Indian trusted in gold, thinking its colour ill-omened. The caribou must never be killed with a wooden implement, since that was unlucky and may keep the herds out of the timber. Before cutting into the carcass, the eye had to be pierced to blind the animal's spirit to the hunter's butchery. Thereafter, every organ of the caribou could be consumed except the lungs. These were absolutely taboo, either as food or for any other use. Not even a dog was allowed to eat them, and they would always be hung carefully in a high tree and left to dry and wither undisturbed.

The most evil spirit known to the Indian was a shadowy, unpropitious spirit-monster called the Weetigo. In snow it could not go abroad in the Barrens without leaving footprints. But in summer, the Weetigo roamed unimpeded and trackless, kept at bay only by the constant burning of camp-fires and lamps. The Dogrib tribe, trusting that the Weetigo could not cross water, liked to camp on an island if they felt danger near. And when an Indian died, the burial took place on a hill, the body lying under a stone cairn and protected by a wooden stockade to defend against attack by wolves and the Weetigo.

Ever since 1907, at Great Bear Lake, the Barren Ground Indians had been central to Jack's view of the North. At times he decried their stubbornness and greed. He abhorred their treatment of dogs. But in all essentials, Jack's ideas about travel in the Barrens were derived from Indian thinking. Rapid movement with minimal loads, living by hunting and trapping alone, knowing the movement of game, sharing food in times of want – all these he had learned from the Indian.

He cultivated many of the natives' everyday habits. He loved to crack open bones with a hammer and suck out the raw marrow. He brewed tea all day long. He used a single unwashed knife for every operation, from eating to butchering. And after relieving himself he cleaned his rump with a stick. One of his acquaintances, Max Cameron, a chief geographer in the Department of Mines, made these comments about Jack from a perspective that is – not unusually for the time – unsympathetic to Indian culture:

> Had he been born an Indian, he would only have been remarkable for his honesty and forthrightness. Being a white man he was remarkable for his Indian characteristics also, i.e. improvidence, periods of intense energy alternating with slovenly, lazy, slipshod periods.

As already noted, Critchell-Bullock's diary of 1924–5 gives the same impression: of a man who was content to slip into a happy-go-lucky Indian style of life, a white man 'gone native'.

The Indianization of a Harrow old boy is of course the very spice of the Hornby legend. He was Gentleman Jack who, in the words of the *Edmonton Journal*, 'could out-run any Indian on the trail, could outlast any Indian in endurance and could outstarve any Indian when there was nothing left but starvation'. But the truth was that no white man – certainly not a proud loner like Jack – could attach himself reliably to the Indians' essential support systems. It is true that the Indians saved him in 1921 when he nearly starved at Fort Reliance. But kinship ties, and the membership of cooperative hunting bands, were a native's insurance against injury, illness or other bad luck. Such cover rarely extended to whites.

8. Hornby's Channel

Adverse northerly winds kept the party pinned back in the Slave River delta for forty-eight hours but, on 10 June, the barometer moderated and they paddled the big canoe out into the Great Slave Lake. The Mission sawmill had represented virtually the last of civilization. Now, only one more white man's outpost lay before them: a shack at Fort Reliance, far away at the east end of the lake, in which stood a single trading depot. But there would be no more missions, no RCMP posts. And beyond Reliance was only the steep ascent to the plateau of northern Canadian tundra – the Barren Ground itself.

Jack is going into a country that has never been trapped by anyone else before because it is too hard to get into with Supplies, and most men take Supplies and dont rely on the Country . . .

In your letter you said keep a diary, and I am, but on a large scale. I have got 3 large notebooks of 200 pages but I can see they wont last more than a few months because there is lots to write about. Of course the more I include the more value. I shall keep count of weather and the movements and habits of animals as well as a sort of natural History report.

All these items count because last time Jack was

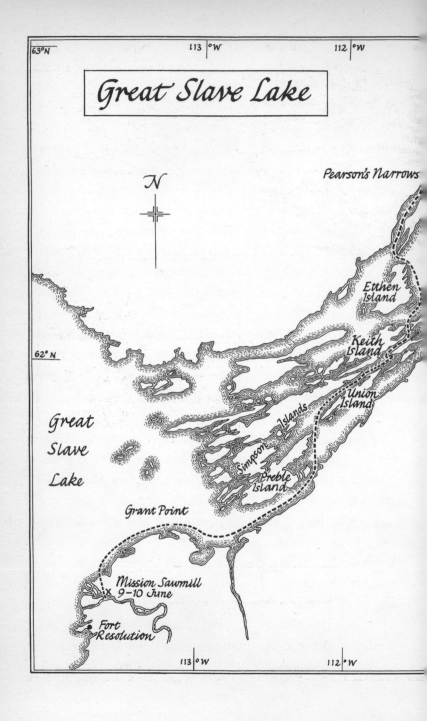

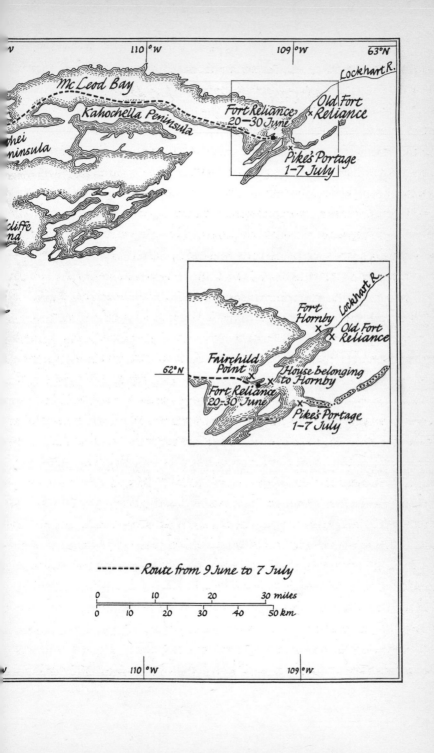

asked by the Government to give a report of the migration of the caribou and he got 600 dollars for it so I shall be prepared for the same.

As if the ordeal ahead were not formidable enough, Harold's letter home, posted like Edgar's from the Mission sawmill, exaggerates the distance still to be travelled to their winter resort.

We are now at Fort Resolution, near Great Slave Lake, having paddled our own canoe most of the way from Edmonton, about six hundred miles so far. We have about 1,500 to go, which will take all summer. In the winter we shall prospect, and, if we do not get out before freeze-up, trap again and get out the following summer by way of the Atlantic coast.

In reality the distance was another six hundred miles; they were, in effect, about halfway into their journey.

The fragment of Harold's letter is especially revealing in its mention of prospecting and fur-trapping – practical reasons for travelling in the Far North. Edgar, although he less frequently mentions mineralogy, writes enthusiastically of furs and scientific discovery. Both sons wanted to impress on their parents that this was a serious trip. Jack encouraged this, telling them to expect good profits from fur and talking up his own prospecting and scientific credentials.

In the first place, his abilities as a prospector were extremely dubious. George Douglas, a skilled mining engineer, wrote unequivocally that Jack 'knew nothing of

geology or prospecting', a view seconded by another northern traveller, William Macdonald.

> Hornby was not a prospector and did not know one
> rock from another. He was, however, interested in
> everything in the country and was always picking up
> unusual coloured rock. In 1922 he had some pieces of
> silver from Great Bear Lake, whether he found the
> silver himself or got it from Indians I cannot say.

If prospecting success would only come Jack's way by accident, trapping ought to have been second nature to him. He
had spent years with Indians and white trappers in the
Barrens, familiarizing himself with different types of trap,
the setting of trap-lines and the habits of the prey, whether
muskrat, arctic fox, wolf or bear. Many years later, C.H.D.
Clarke, who knew the Thelon as well as anyone, claimed
that 'Hornby was certainly proficient as a fox-trapper.' Yet
he never in his whole career made any money from furs. The
trapping-and-trading scheme in which he assisted Cosmo
Melvill in 1908–10 had been a failure and, even when Jack
took over all the departing Melvill's traps, he could make no
better use of them by himself.

During Jack's 1924–5 winter above Fort Reliance with
Critchell-Bullock, it had been important that they get a
commercial quantity of fur – the economics of the trip
demanded it. But, once out in his favourite country, Jack
could never concentrate on any job for long, as Critchell-
Bullock's diary repeatedly shows – as, for example, in an
entry dated 15 March 1925:

Cannot imagine what H. is up to. Here we are, dozens of foxes behind the other people [trapping in the area] & he is still wandering about. We ought to get in a month's supply of wood and settle down to work. Again, he will set a line of traps, spend days doing it & never trouble to look at it. [He should] Put down the traps where they are close enough to look at.

Even more galling for Critchell-Bullock was the discovery they made at journey's end, when the pelts had

so deteriorated on reaching civilization as to be worthless. This was due to the fact that candles ran out, wolf and fox fat had to be used instead, and the light provided was so poor as to render careful cleaning impossible. During the summer's heat the [residue of] grease 'boiled' into the hide and loosened the fur.

It was a disaster no competent trapper would have let happen.
  Finally, could Jack have compiled a 'sort of natural History report'? His Caribou Report, though informative, had been anything but statistical. And although he was interested in, and observant of, nature, this came in strange fits and was entirely unmethodical. As Critchell-Bullock wrote:

Although starving and hardly able to stand, he would often dig for hours to uncover a rodent, his tools, for want of anything better, usually being an axe and a gold pan.

Hornby of the North, in mid-1919 at Fort Norman,
studying the Hudson's Bay Company catalogue.

Staff and pupils at the Grange School, Folkestone, 1921.
Edgar Christian is in row three, third from the left, and headmaster
C. H. Wodeman in row two, seventh from the left.

Bron Dirion, the Christians' country home in North Wales.

The Christian family at the seaside, North Wales.

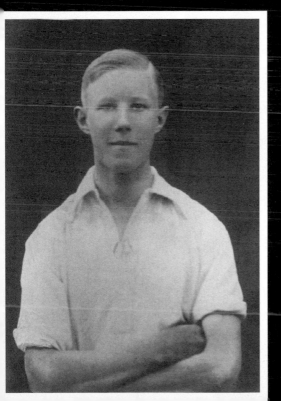

Sixteen-year-old Edgar, at Dover College.

Harold Adlard in flyer's uniform.

Harold in 1918–20, with walking stick, a possible consequence of his flying injury.

Harold in Canada, 1923–6.

View by Captain Critchell-Bullock of Mount Coleman, in the Rockies, where he and Jack made a trial excursion in 1923, before their Barren Lands trip.

Critchell-Bullock ready for the trail, Mount Coleman.

Critchell-Bullock in caribou-skin parka.

View of the Mount Coleman camp.

*Jack brewing tea,
Mount Coleman.*

Eskimo on the Mackenzie River.

Arimo, who nursed Jack back to health on Great Bear Lake. For this woman he conceived a great affection. She later became Mrs D'Arcy Arden.

White-faced musk-oxen in defensive formation.

Jack cleaning wolverine skin in 1924.
Two years later, this would be his only food.

The north end of Artillery Lake, looking south, autumn 1924.

Jack cracking bones for marrow.

Jack, with Whitey, launching a loaded canoe on the Thelon, 1925.

Artefacts presented by Jack to the National Museum, Ottowa.

Jack portaging under a maximum load.

APRIL 1924
XXXXXXXXXXXXXXXXX

<u>April 1st</u> This month has started i
none too good, we had to Eat
Wolverine hide for Supper. Storm
hard all day & we could do noth
much. Jack took a walk to creek
located hare trail & set a trap w
I hope to visit tommorrow. Jack is
suffering agonies in left leg whi
must make Life absolute hell u
the present Conditions. Harold gett
wood & water & says he feels rotten
do we! S.W. strong. −20 −11°.
<u>April 2nd</u> Milder weather seem
to have come along to day which i
hope will improve matters. Jack
took a walk to where Caribou was
killed in February to bring in pau
he managed to collect a little ble
which made an Excellent snack
I went up Creek to look at
hare trap but nothing. Set 1 mo

A page from Edgar's Diary.

trap & hunted Ptarmigan
h seem to have fed Everywhere
otherwise are not to be seen
-Harold is feeling weak getting
& I hope we get food soon.
a suffering agonies from
les in left leg probably a
e in weather causing it.
morrow I hope to set 2 have
down River & 2 fox traps
ame time see if any
upon an Island. —20.0 N.E.
l 3rd Another fruitless & very
issappointing day. Instead of
d weather this morning it was
wing hard from N.E. & clear
. Jack's leg is still very painful
gets little sleep. we slept on
late to day being very tired
night & we had breakfast
prepare from Wolverine hide
got out meal at noon & then
lked to the Creek to look at

Cabin on the Thelon, built by Jack, Harold and Edgar in October–November 1926.

Graves dug by RCMP patrol, June 1928.

At other times, he could give a passable impression of a besotted lepidopterist.

> H. amused himself most of the morning madly chasing butterflies. He was most amusing. Suddenly he would drop a huge pack and with a net about his own size go hurtling over rocks, through muskeg and willows.

However, Jack's interest was neither sustained nor systematic enough to be scientific.

> Later, more often than not, he would lose his specimens in a capsized canoe, in a blown-down tent, or forget them at some camp.

Summing up Jack as a collector of data in general, Douglas downgrades him to a 'beachcomber'. Critchell-Bullock is even more scathing about his scientific pretensions:

> Except for a few specimens collected when with Critchell-Bullock, he contributed to science nothing thatscience did not already know about the flora and fauna of the Far North.

These 'few specimens' were sometimes given to Dr R. M. Anderson, Head of Biology at the National Museum in Ottowa. But, as Anderson remembers, these were items of minimal value such as 'mummified and mouldy mice without data out of the pockets of his best suit'.

The truth is that there were no practical purposes behind

this Thelon journey. Far from the considerations of commerce and science, it was impelled by almost entirely personal motives peculiar to Jack Hornby.

The Great Slave Lake is a vast inland sea of almost ten thousand square miles. As a waterway it is not to be treated lightly. Violent squalls could whip the surface into a heavy breaking swell which caught out and capsized many northern travellers, sending outfits and precious furs to the bottom and, as likely as not, marooning the wayfarers themselves on one of the lake's innumerable stony red granite islands. At first, these were the conditions Jack's party encountered in June 1926. Their leader pushed them to extremes of endurance, paddling on one occasion for a day and a night. The going was tough and – with rations already limited – Edgar was hungry.

> In my letter to Mother I said we had some Pemican with us. It may sound crude as I thought at first. I did not look forward to a meal of Hard Tack biscuits and Pemican and tea without milk until I had been Paddling a Laden Canoe for 5 hours and then by Jove I was ready for any damn thing and thoroughly Enjoyed it.

Pemmican, the staple trail food of travellers in the North, had been used from ancient times in North America as a way of compacting and storing protein. It was prepared in summer. A thick haunch of a large animal – buffalo, moose, musk-ox or caribou – was trimmed and rotated in one hand as, with a sharp blade, a continuous slab of meat was peeled from it, as if unfolding a bedroll. These broad slabs of meat, looking like gargantuan steaks, were draped high on a willow-stick frame and air-cured for four or five days, until hard and crisp. Then, to make the pemmican, the dried meat was pounded to a powder with stones, mixed with grease to form a paste and flavoured with dried blueberries, raisins or even sugar. When writing of this legendary food, Edgar's enthusiasm begins to read like advertising copy.

> Pemican has great nourishment in it and you can go on Pemican much Longer than on any other thing I have eaten yet. In the middle of our 24 hours Paddle at times we got tired but after Pemican I felt a different person altogether.

This diet was augmented with bannocks. The bannock, a simple flour-and-water cake, pan-fried or roasted in embers, was the staple method of consuming flour in the Barren Ground. It was the trappers' bread.

Meanwhile, the canoeists struggled through harsh and windy waters along the south shore, passing the mouth of the Talston River, which flowed into the lake at this point. The Talston is a long, serviceable canoe route into good trapping country. Jack had once 'attempted to run a very bad rapid on the Talston and lost his outfit. Very nearly starved.' One or two isolated trappers' cabins were visible ashore as they pressed on to Pearson's Narrows. Jack was now navigating the same waters as those of his sketch-map, made for Guy Blanchet on the schooner *Ptarmigan* four

years earlier. The sketch had been intended to illustrate
the complicated system of islands and mazy peninsulas that
confuses the eastern end of the lake, until the broad sweep
of McLeod Bay offers a clear, curved course into Fort
Reliance. In the central section of Jack's route, the canoeists
needed to thread between close-set islands. They would
travel at night, when the wind dropped, or otherwise hug
the southern shores of Preble Island (which Hornby knew
as 'Rabbit Island'), the Simpson Islands ('Barquisht Island')
and Keith Island, in order to shelter from the vicious north-
westerly blow. It was the channel Blanchet had named
Hornby Channel but of which, on his sketch, Hornby was
even more possessive: he called it 'Hornby's Channel'.

On 12 June, as the sun lowered itself behind a liquid
horizon, they veered away from the shore at last and made
for Pearson's Narrows.

The Lake looked very pretty with the setting sun on
the horizon. I was now beginning to enjoy the trip
because of the Scenery & Surroundings which are
wonderful. It is a great sensation to be paddling along
over the rolling water without a sound Except that
caused by wildlife. The ducks were flying here and
there and Loons were whistling in the distance and the
water sounding on the shore which we were steadily
drawing away from.

About 2 a.m. we were often being surprised by
birds called Arctic terns. They seemed to appear from
nowhere because they are all white and you can't see
them or hear them coming but when they see you they

just make a bother all the time by swooping down and pecking your hat or your head. They are very plucky and treacherous little devils and one soon dislikes them however nice they may look when flying.

Our first island was all rock with just a tuft of grass here and there and in all about 1 acre in size. There were lots of nests on the island judging by the number of terns and gulls which were flying around, so we pulled in lighted a fire and started a search for eggs which would make 'un bon repas'. We found lots of terns' nests, and the eggs are just like plovers in England. We found 31 tern eggs and Jack found a ducks nest of 11, so we were eager to get our feet in the trough. By testing in water the ducks eggs seemed OK but my word when I cracked one open there was a loud report and lots of odour so we took back all the other eggs to the nest. All the terns eggs were just as disappointing and we only had 6 between us. What a feast we might have had if we had not been held up by winds a week before.

They were on a north-eastern course and island-hopping, as the wind shifted round to the south. But once through the Narrows, at about 3.30 a.m., their course altered northerly and, with the wind behind, they were able to set the sail.

Sailing is simply A.1. when the wind is moderate and does not make the water all choppy and the canoe roll. One can lie back under the canvas covering with the sun shining on your face and just take it easy and feel

yourself gliding along making much better time than
having to pull hard at the paddle all the time. When we
sail I always thoroughly enjoy life and just lie and think
of B.D. and wish you were all here to enjoy what I do.
So far on the trip we have not caught any fish so Jack
said put out a troll to see if we could hook a trout. It
happened that we were sailing too fast to fish just then,
but when we had to put down the sail after the wind
dropped I had a line tied to my leg, and within a
minute or so of paddling I felt a jerk and knew our next
meal was caught. Of course when I saw the fish I said
it was a beauty, a trout weighing 6 lbs, but Jack said it
was a rotten fish not worth keeping. I couldn't understand him saying this but I soon learned the difference
between a poor fish and a good one regardless of size
altogether . . . We cooked the trout that evening and I
thought it was the best fish I ever had and couldn't be
better, but I had yet to learn what a good piece of fish
was.

A 'good piece of fish' was represented by their breakfast,
caught in a shore-net during the night – three trout of 10 lb
each and 'three whitefish, which Jack says is a kind of dace
in England'. In the morning Jack took time to show Edgar
and Harold how best to handle the shore net and they only
re-embarked at midday, paddling for seven hours with just
the one 'spell' for a late lunch of cold trout.

Next day, they sailed again. This time Edgar lay watching
the white clouds scudding past overhead, and fell asleep.

When I awoke the sail was just about to be taken down as the wind had dropped and we were in lea of some islands. While we were paddling we could see away in front 2 bald headed eagles flying round and Jack said they must have had a nest somewhere close by. The birds did not seem to be very large at first sight but when we got closer they certainly looked fine, flying round in the sun which showed their markings very vividly, white head, yellow bill and white tail and the rest all brownish red.

The bald eagle, as his reading of *The Birds of Eastern Canada* would have told Edgar, is a waterside bird of prey, with a six-foot wingspan – the largest in north America. It is a fish-eater that also consumes smaller birds and mammals. The sighting of a nesting pair was exciting for, as P. A. Taverner says, 'though once a typical species of the eastern landscape, it is yearly growing rarer, until now in most localities the sight of one is an event of some importance'.

They spotted an island on which stood a tall spruce, with a mess of twigs, feathers and balls of fur around its base, and clearly saw the great eagle's nest laid among the highest branches. It brought a characteristically boyish response from Jack, who announced he would climb the tree. After an arduous ascent with the Kodak slung from his neck and the tree bending and swaying in the gale, Jack peered over the rim of the nest. He called down that there were two fledglings, gaping at him with open beaks. As Jack took photographs, Edgar watched the flustered parents wheeling anxiously around 'making a weird noise. The best way I can explain the noise is that it was just like a farm cart with unoiled wheels coming along.'

After this they spelled, ate and pushed off again, conscious of delay but feeling 'the satisfaction of knowing the photo would be valuable if it came out well'. They had not been paddling long when they spotted another canoe coming towards them, the first they had seen since the Mission mill. It contained four 'sweedish' men, trappers returning to Fort Resolution to sell their catch and, in the accepted custom of the time, they beached their canoes at the nearest island and passed an hour together over tea, a meal and the exchange of news. Frustratingly, Edgar does not say what was learned about trapping and hunting conditions further east, but he found them 'jolly good chaps'. Jack, of course, had known the men for years.

Continuing the next day, they noticed smoke ashore rising beside a beached scow, a wide, flat-bottomed boat capable of carrying a much larger payload than any canoe. They paddled towards it and found a family of Indians on the look-out for Scotty Robb, the trader, whose motor boat they hoped would give them a tow as far as his newly established post at Reliance. Edgar, prompted by Jack, shook hands solemnly with all the Indians, which 'pleased them immensely, because . . .' – with this word, at the end of its fourteenth page, Edgar's narrative breaks off. Except for some rapid notes about Pike's Portage, that is the last from Edgar until he takes up his diary almost three months later.

We know that they waited with the scow and, when Robb turned up, Jack took the opportunity to attach his own group to the tow party. Reliance was still more than fifty miles away and Robb's engine would considerably speed them along. During the journey, they came upon another party of trappers with a broken outboard engine and these, too, were brought under tow. Now this small train of boats was chugging beneath the dramatic beetling cliffs which swept in a huge arc around the north of McLeod Bay. Jack could nudge Edgar, point to the skyline, hundreds of feet above them, and say this was the lip of the Barren Ground itself. Tracing the sheer rock face down to the shore, the eye picked out nests of gulls and hawks and then, at the bottom, vast blocks of ice piled upon the shingle beaches, shuffled ashore by the south-westerly wind to melt slowly in the sun.

Closer still to Reliance, they encountered a further succession of trappers coming towards them with their winter's catch of fur. Some – Matt Murphy, F. L. Buckley – had been working the pelts in this area for years. One of the oddest was Jim Cooley, an unmistakable figure sitting bolt upright in his canoe, always concerned to look smart in a tailored blue serge suit and grey stetson. Finally, they came upon the Stewart brothers, Jack's particular friends. They turned their craft around when they saw Jack who, casting loose his own canoe, paddled back with them to Fairchild Point.

Settling down for a long conversation, the Stewarts must have told of hunting and trapping conditions the previous winter in the Barrens – not as far as the Thelon valley but certainly in the country to the north-east of Reliance, around Artillery Lake. They apparently also discussed stores. Malcolm Stewart later said that he looked over Jack's edible supplies and told him he should get more from Scotty Robb. Jack said he needed nothing.

In fact the problem was money and, when Malcolm Stewart offered to settle the bill, Jack accepted. In this way, vital additional bags of tea, flour and sugar were acquired. The Stewarts then left for Fort Resolution, but said they would be returning for the winter. Jack told them he would see them on the Thelon. It was now 21 June.

9. Reliance

Scotty Robb's depot stood on Fairchild Point, on the tip of the more northerly of two spits of land which reach towards each other, almost enclosing what Jack called Hornby's Bay. Near the depot stood a second (as marked on his sketch map) 'house belonging to Hornby', which Jack had used during the grim winter of 1921–2, when he dragged himself from fishing hole to fishing hole on hands and knees and became mentally unhinged by his privation.

In winter it was a desperately cold and dangerous place, as the naval explorer George Back had discovered in the mid-1830s, leaving a clump of ruined chimney stacks to testify to his two starving winters there. But relatively few of the early travellers knew this darker side of Fort Reliance. In summer, what struck them above all was its extraordinary beauty. J. W. Tyrrell found it one of the most beautiful spots he had ever seen in the north, with lovely green slopes rising high from the lake shore in regular and beautiful terraces to a height of two hundred feet. And when camped there in August 1925 with Hornby, Critchell-Bullock, too, found himself transported by an enchantment worthy of Prospero's island. In one passage from *An Expedition* he writes of the curious utopian reveries that enraptured him.

My health had returned due to a combination of nature's food, unlimited exercise and a pure atmosphere and I commenced to speculate on the future of this pleasant spot. I remembered the war casualties and I pictured Fort Reliance as a great sanatorium to which they could come to recuperate mentally and physically. I fancy I saw a great caribou ranch on Artillery Lake, and these men, living in log cabins about Charlton Harbour, assisting with the herding, fishing and hunting and eating the superb flesh of the early autumn 'bulls'. I visualized a great ranch industry growing up but running sweetly because of its philanthropic quality. I imagined white fox farms coming into their own, the prohibition of the steel trap, and the Indians leading useful, happier lives.

This passage is from an early draft of the report and, strikingly, 'war casualties' are replaced in the final version by 'men I had seen suffering from tropical diseases'. Critchell-Bullock had contracted malaria in Syria. The only war casualty to hand was Jack Hornby. Perhaps he concluded that, while he himself could benefit from the salubrious air at Reliance, Jack was incurable.

Whether it was under the magic influence of Fort Reliance, or for more prosaic reasons, Jack at the end of June 1926 seems to have been in the mood to dawdle. In truth, while there had been earlier worries about the schedule, the expedition could now afford a little lingering. They were well up to time. On the Barrens the thaw was still underway and, with no dogs or sleds, they would not make progress until the ice cleared. Jack probably also wanted to show his companions Back's chimneys as well as to visit Fort Hornby and an equipment cache which he had erected during his later stay with Critchell-Bullock.

The monuments were about eight miles from Fairchild, at the landward end of the spit. The 1924 cache was nearby, a large hutch raised on poles to deter spoiling by animals and containing Critchell-Bullock's excess scientific equipment and other gear. When the captain was holed up in the Barrens throughout the winter of 1924–5, he had been continually irked by Jack's steadfast refusal to fetch up his meteorological instruments, clean underwear and spare toothbrush from here. In 1926 the stores were presumably still in place and, if they included anything Jack might need on the Thelon, he would have to break into the cache. It may, of course, have already been violated by Indians, trappers or the elements.

There were also Indian encampments to visit, if only to have snowshoes and spare moccasins made by the squaws. The days of Franklin and Back in their nailed boots were gone and trappers had long taken to the Indian fashion in winter footwear. Worn over a thick woollen sock known as a duffel, the moccasin took the approximate shape of a ballet shoe, with a round toe and high heel-piece bound with a lace of babiche around the front of the ankle. Upper and sole were both made from moose or caribou leather, not only tanned but smoked, making it soft and flexible enough to keep the muscles of the foot moving and warm. The fact that moccasins were permeable to water was not much of an issue in regions where, during winter, the snow and ice never thawed. Four pairs would see a man through until spring.

By distributing one's weight evenly across a broad surface, snowshoes make it possible to walk across the top of the snow without breaking through its crust. Around two feet long, the Barren Ground shoe was shorter than the woodland variety by about eight inches. In plan it was the shape of an exceptionally wide-bellied canoe. Two flexible birch or spruce-wood poles were spliced together at their extremities and forced apart in the middle by a pair of thwarts. The shoe was therefore pointed at both ends, its nose bent upwards in a prow and its frame filled in with a tight mesh of babiche. The wearer's feet were bound tightly to this web by more babiche or leather thongs.

Jack did not like snowshoes and, according to Critchell-Bullock, wore them rarely because his 'tender feet' were rubbed by the laces. But those feet were large enough, and their owner small enough, to enable him to travel without snowshoes across most snow, while more heavily built men (like the captain himself) used snowshoes virtually every time they went out in winter. If the shoes' strength and lightness were not to be compromised, they had to be made with Indian expertise. Lightness was a prerequisite but so was solid construction. One of the most time-consuming tasks in a winter camp was the repair of snowshoes constantly damaged by contact with sharp rocks, tree stumps and ice.

Edgar watched the Indians. He drank tea with them and observed the women who cut and sewed the footwear using wooden-handled steel knives and bone needles. The squaws not engaged in work would pick through their children's scalps for lice, cracking them between their teeth before swallowing them with all the appearance of relish.

It is not clear how long Jack, Harold and Edgar rested at Fairchild Point. Writing a letter from the Barrens dated 12 August, Harold said that they had still been on Great Slave Lake 'at the end of July', but he also states this was 'a whole month ago', which suggests an accidental substitution of July for June. If so, it was after no more than two weeks that Jack brought the summer idyll at Reliance to an end and packed for Pike's Portage and the Barren Ground. He knew he could not afford to wait too long. If they travelled no faster than he had with Critchell-Bullock, arrival at their chosen winter quarters on the Thelon might be three months away. So now, some time after the middle of the month, they canoed across the breadth of 'Hornby's' bay and landed at the foot of Pike's Portage.

Pike's Portage is the one relatively easy point of entry to the Barrens from Reliance. George Back had had real trouble going in via the turbulent, 'toilsome' Hoarfrost River to the west, and found it no less difficult returning down the dangerous rapids of the Lockhart River, plunging into the lake at Fort Reliance itself. Pike's Portage is much easier than either of these ways. It is named after the English adventurer and amateur man of letters Warburton Pike, who had come up to the Barren Ground from the west in 1889, with the young James Mackinlay, an old friend of Jack.

After canoeing to the bottom of the portage, a spot on the shore about thirty miles from Fairchild Point, the travellers were faced with a stiff two-mile climb to a height of about three hundred feet. Every piece of their cargo would have to be walked to the top in back-packs, and the canoe hauled over birch-pole rollers. From there a gentler slope led another three miles to the first of a chain of eight small lakes, which took them in turn to the much larger Artillery Lake. From here they would be paddling forward into the Barrens themselves.

A reminder of how the North was changing – naturally a quite unwelcome one to Jack – came when they met a different type of traveller camped at the foot of the portage. These were the men of a geodetic survey party, studying the complicated, still not completely mapped shoreline of the Great Slave Lake. One of them, Stan Carpenter, later recalled that Jack and his party seemed 'completely devoid of food other than tea' – a detail which, although not true, shows Jack's myth-making at work. Looking over the incomparably better-equipped outfit of the government team, Jack would undoubtedly have boasted that he had little need of superfluities, but emulated the Indian by taking no supplies except tea and living off the land. Such assertions were his customary way of claiming superiority over this new breed of 'official' explorers who, with their technologies, removed all the mystery and excitement from the Barren Ground.

Once the climb had been completed, the distance to the southern end of Artillery Lake was about twenty-five miles, of which almost twenty were covered by water along the chain of lakes. After the tough initial ascent, the eight remaining portages were measured in hundreds of yards and the landscape was exceptionally beautiful. It teemed with plant life – good tree cover on the surrounding hillsides and berries along the lakes' sandy banks. The shrub *Ledum Ericaceae*, 'Labrador tea', showed its small, white, clustered flowers abundantly in the muskeg, as did the dwarf rhododendron Lapland rosebay, with its deep pink blooms. Yet, a mere foot beneath their roots, lay the permafrost.

Pike's Portage, with its first introduction to back-breaking labour and its altered topography, was a reminder that from here on they must be entirely self-reliant, as there would be no more trading posts, no cabins ready-made to shelter them, no convenient caches. At some point during the portage, the point was underlined by a meeting with a Swedish trapper named Fred Lind, who was on his way in the opposite direction out of the Artillery Lake trapping grounds, which he had been working all winter and spring. Lind later reported that, seeing the three men had no food (he must have meant no fresh meat), he had fed them. He became the last man they spoke to on the way to the Barrens.

At the extremities of the portage, Pike and Mackinlay had made lop-sticks. This is a type of landmark conventionally used by Northern explorers – a tall pine, from which the boughs were chopped off with only a star-spray of branches left at the top to form an easily recognizable marker. The lop-sticks still stood and, in their trunks, Pike's and Mackinlay's carved names were clearly visible. It should have taken Jack, Edgar and Harold less than a week to reach the upper lop-stick. For the first, stiff climb, two or three days were enough, allowing perhaps seven or eight individual packs apiece and a single hard haul by all three men to move the canoe. Another two or three days would then be enough to see them safely camped and ready to launch on to Artillery Lake. But it was high summer, and the freeze-up was six to eight weeks away. Lack of meat and sightings of caribou might have tempted Jack to stay and hunt.

Specimens of Barren Ground caribou, *Rangifer Arcticus*, found at Artillery at this date would all have been bulls, their horns perhaps just still 'in velvet'. At the end of the previous autumn's rut the herd as a whole had wintered within the tree-line, before the cows re-migrated in vast herds over a distance as great as seven hundred miles to the Arctic Ocean, where they threw their calves in early June. At this time of year, well over half a million beasts were on the move, but most of the bulls remained in the south, scattered at random throughout the woods that fringed the Barren Ground. Here, along a thousand-mile front, they patiently awaited the return of the cows, before moving out of the woods in late August to meet them in the Barren Ground for rutting. The cycle then repeated itself.

In early July, the bull caribou around Artillery Lake were of this type. They were probably neither numerous nor perfect for eating, although they would have been picking up condition fast. Nor were they particularly easy prey. Although short-sighted, the caribou has excellent hearing and an acute sense of smell. The hunting of these isolated individuals (as opposed to shooting into migrating herds) demands the same approach as deer-stalking in a Scottish glen – knowledge, patience, luck and good shooting. The rifleman must get as close as possible from downwind before loosing off a shot. The caribou can be slow to react to a sudden danger but, when it does move, flight is swift. However, if the animal scents the predator from a distance, it will move off more slowly. It is then well worth following because, rather than escaping like most deer into the tree-cover, the nervous caribou has a tendency to head towards open ground. Here it may well present a target for a clear shot of between three and five hundred yards.

Indeed, the hunter who shoots over long range can sometimes bag two, three or even four caribou in a few seconds – a feat Jack himself is reputed to have managed. It is possible because, if one of a small group of animals is picked off from a distance, the others will merely stand and look curiously at their fallen comrade and can themselves be shot in turn. But this requires very accurate, very rapid shooting – a succession of instant kills – since a wounded caribou that runs takes his companions with him. In this case the blood trail must be followed as hard and as fast as the hunter can manage, in a chase that continues until the hunted – or the hunter – is exhausted.

Jack must often in his life have found it necessary to run down a wounded caribou. He had remarkable stamina, but was not conspicuous for his patience or careful methods, and accounts by his friends the Douglas brothers of his marksmanship suggest much inconsistency. Lionel Douglas called his rifle shooting 'erratic' and 'wild', and even the more sympathetic George never considered Jack an effective hunter, if only because he would not look after his gun.

H. couldn't even clean his rifle. [Once] I had the curiosity to look through the barrel, it was heavily 'leaded' and rusty.

On the other hand, given a serviceable weapon, Jack could perform like a dead shot. On one occasion, Critchell-Bullock's diary reports, 'H. made a fine shot five hundred yards with the Ross. Killed a cow in one shot.' It was also Critchell-Bullock who reported that Jack had felled four caribou with four consecutive shots, though he does not give the range.

So, however well he could shoot under ideal conditions, Douglas's judgement is probably right about Jack's performance as a hunter. Suppose they did break off at Artillery to 'blood' Edgar and Harold, this might have been a process spread over several precious days – time that Jack might have more wisely spent hurrying up the lake and into the Barren Ground, where he could expect to intercept the herds as they migrated south.

The Artillery Lake stretch must have had Edgar thinking of home and family. It had been named by Back to honour the spirit of 'the distinguished corps to which some of my crew belonged' – a corps to which Edgar himself, the son of a gunnery colonel, was also strongly tied. But more ancient spirits than the Royal Artillery brooded over these waters, two of the most powerful being vested in a pair of landmarks, some twenty miles up the lake on the south side, between which all canoeists must pass. On the eastern side was 'Rat Lodge', a high dolomite hill, dropping sheer down to the water; on the west was 'Beaver Lodge', a drift hill at the end of a long, low point. According to Indian belief, a giant spectral rat, the embodiment of treachery, inhabited Rat Lodge, while a malevolent beaver-spirit lived within the dolomite rock. Every passing Indian made propitiatory gestures towards these baleful presences, sometimes in the form of offerings cast into the water, hoping to ward off the ill-luck of crossing this line across the lake. Retribution by the Beaver and the Rat was believed to take the form of drastic storms and adverse winds. It was a cautionary superstition because, although on a map this looks hardly more than a scrap of water next to the vastness of Great Slave Lake, Artillery is fifty miles long and subject to vicious, unpredictable changes of weather. Damage from rough water then becomes difficult to escape, even ashore. As Critchell-Bullock tells it:

> Though the lake is quite narrow we found that the water during a gale would become piled up on the weather shore to a considerable height, and during one night in particular it necessitated thrice removing our entire belongings in all fifty feet further inland.

Although moving up the lake several weeks earlier than was the case with Critchell-Bullock and Jack in 1924, the 1926 expedition does not seem (on all the evidence) to have struck luckier. It may even have been held up by ice jams still clogging the channel. At this higher altitude, Artillery was certainly colder and wilder than Reliance and becoming progressively more so as they headed north. On the western side of the lake, they could see that trees were plentiful, but along the eastern shore the tree cover became increasingly sparse. Some days before, they had moved into the area of permafrost. Now, looking from the canoe at the north-eastern horizon, Edgar could see just a bare ridge, fuzzed by scrub and stunted pines. They were crossing the tree-line – the last defining boundary of the Barren Ground. And with that crossing came exposure to Barren Ground weather systems, with their ferocious, changeable, predatory winds and their sudden drops in temperature.

Into the northerly end of Artillery flowed the Casba River, which connected it to the shorter, narrower Ptarmigan Lake. Here stood the Stewart Brothers' old cabin and, ten miles inland, dug into the side of an esker, the hole which Jack and Critchell-Bullock had enlarged and fashioned into their bleak winter house. Somewhere around here Jack, Harold and Edgar lingered again, fishing and hunting bull caribou while they coped with the assaults of the blackfly and the difficult weather. Jack may have had a reason to make deliberately slow progress. He knew the Stewarts would be following behind him and, remembering the support they had provided in the past, he may have wanted to give Malcolm and Allan a chance to catch up.

But eventually Jack abandoned that prospect. He loaded the canoe and set off once again up the Casba. At the top of it was a portage round some rapids before they could launch themselves upon Ptarmigan Lake. Following northern tradition, Jack built a cairn beside these rapids and produced an old tin box in which snuff had once been sold, placing a note inside. It was addressed to the Stewart brothers:

Travelling slowly. Flies bad. Shot a fat buck caribou. Hope to see you down the Hanbury this winter.

The note had been dated but, when the Stewarts duly found and copied it, they failed to make a record of that date. It must, however, have been about 30 July.

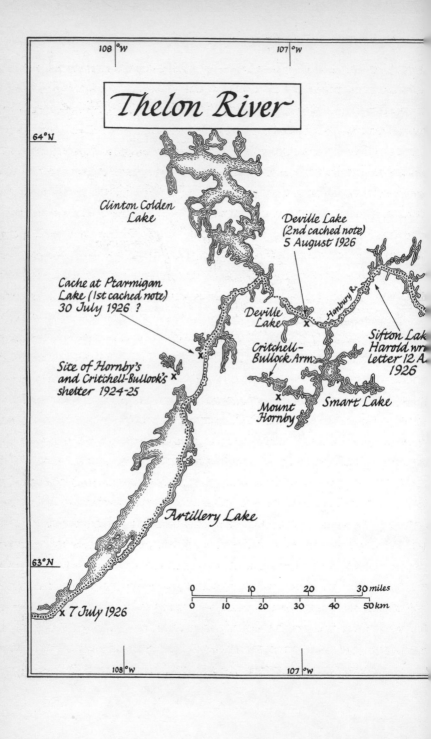

Thelon River

108 °W   107 °W

64°N

Clinton Colden Lake

Deville Lake (2nd cached note) 5 August 1926

Cache at Ptarmigan Lake (1st cached note) 30 July 1926 ?

Deville Lake

Critchell-Bullock Arm

Hanbury R.

Sifton Lak Harold wr letter 12 A 1926

Site of Hornby's and Critchell-Bullock's shelter 1924-25

Mount Hornby

Smart Lake

Artillery Lake

63°N

x 7 July 1926

0   10   20   30 miles
0   10   20   30   40   50 km

108 °W   107 °W

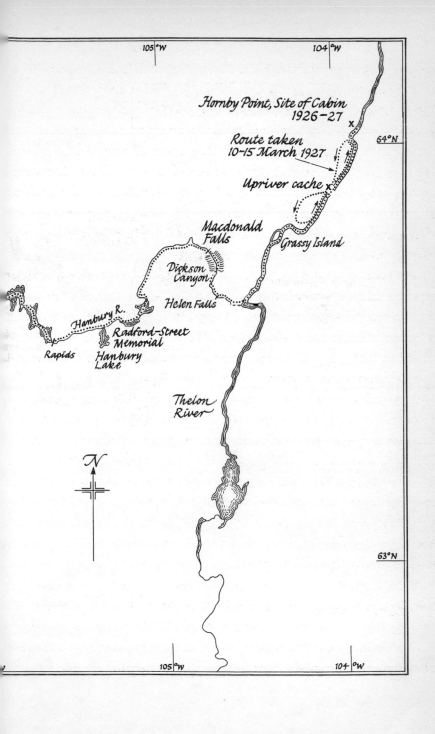

Hornby Point, Site of Cabin
1926–27 ✗

Route taken
10–15 March 1927

Upriver cache ✗

105°W   104°W   64°N

Macdonald
Falls

Dickson
Canyon   Grassy Island

Helen Falls

Hanbury R.

Radford–Street
Memorial

Rapids   Hanbury
Lake

Thelon
River

N

105°W   104°W   63°N

10. Barren Ground

It was the second time Jack had left Artillery Lake and made for the Thelon River by way of the Hanbury, but this time his route would be more straightforward. The previous year, he and Critchell-Bullock had attempted an experimental corner-cutting itinerary, striking directly east from the Casba across the Barren Ground towards Smart Lake, which formed part of the upper Hanbury. But, though it seemed at the outset such a good idea, this had led them close to disaster.

This year, Jack was opting for the route that David Hanbury had first used in 1899, when travelling in the other direction. This was also the way which the surveyor J. W. Tyrrell — the author of Jack's maps — had taken the next year when going from west to east, and which Hanbury took again in the same direction in 1901. The route involved canoeing from the Casba north-east to the top of Ptarmigan Lake and, after meeting a branch of the Hanbury where it flowed into Clinton Colden Lake, turning south-east and (for the time being) upstream towards Deville Lake.

The further north and east they went, the more they penetrated into the wilderness known to the Indians as *de-chin-u-le* — 'the stickless land'. In spite of the fact that, in sheltered places, isolated 'groves' of heavily stunted trees occasionally stubble the ground, this is a more accurate label than 'the Barrens'. Far from barren, the million square miles of Canadian tundra is, all in all, a surprisingly diverse eco-system. Critchell-Bullock records forty-nine species of bird, most of which must also have found their way into Edgar's own (now lost) ornithological checklist. They included the rough-legged hawk, peregrine falcon, gyrfalcon, snowy owl, saw-whet owl, raven, snow goose, Canada goose, white-fronted goose, whistling swan, sandhill crane, duck, ptarmigan, American robin, all four species of loon or diver, horned lark, Canada jay, gulls, sandpipers and sparrows. Most of these come to the Arctic to breed: only a very small number – the ptarmigan, owls, falcons and ravens – actually winter in the Barren Ground. The land in summer also supports almost five hundred ferns, flowering plants and shrubs such as heathers, willows and sorrels, as well as the countless mosses and lichens which provide animal food all the year round.

The fauna which survive around the tree-line and into the Barren Ground – at least seventy-five species of mammal – perpetually fluctuate in number. Beaver are rare at this latitude but muskrats thrive even in winter, their lodges safe beneath the sheet ice which they puncture with 'push-ups' to give access to the open air. But in spring and autumn, when it briefly thaws and refreezes, the lake-water floods over the ice and the rats are forced out, to die and be eaten in their thousands by foxes and wolverines. The tundra mice and lemmings are a less obvious presence. Although reputed by legend to throw themselves over cliffs in acts of migratory mass suicide, lemmings are seen in quantity only when their numbers have outgrown the food supply. It is then that they swarm about in search of sustenance and living space and, in the process, often fall from cliffs and drown in rivers. The Arctic ground squirrel, hare and snowshoe rabbit, culled by predators like the fox and the lynx as well as by weather and periodic disease, are a relatively uncommon sight, although, like the lemming, their populations are subject to unpredictable peaks and troughs. The odd porcupine, too, somehow gets a living, if not in the tundra, then at least close to it. But this secretive creature would normally come to a man's attention only when his dog returns to camp with quills bristling from its nose.

The tundra wolf is a different matter. It is both seen and heard everywhere. There have been many misguided human attempts to reduce its numbers but, in spite of these, and by contrast with the boom-and-bust rodents, the wolf maintains its population in a steady state. Living for most of the year on caribou, it leads a restless, nomadic existence in close symbiosis with its prey. The wolves are organized in small, family-based packs which, in Jack's experience, never rose above seven individuals. The pack is a hierarchy, led by a dominant breeding male. There may be a couple of females, while a younger male relative often runs with them, along with last season's juveniles. Wolves only den up during the breeding season, from mid-May to mid-August, when typically only one of the females will whelp. If caribou are locally unavailable during this time, the wolves and their cubs — between two and four in the litter — subsist on lemming, shrew, eggs, carrion and even insects.

But during its nine months of winter roaming, the tundra wolf is exclusively a caribou eater. Constantly on the move, and consuming anything up to 20 lb of meat per wolf per day, a pack may slaughter ten or more caribou in a week. On this nutritious, fat diet it becomes a sleek and powerful predator with a propensity, like the Indian, for overkill.

It hunts alone or in a pack. The caribou is stalked using any available cover. When close enough, the wolf or wolves sprint into the herd, snapping, dodging and feinting. When a few individuals are separated from the herd, one is selected, tripped and has its throat torn open, an action repeated until several caribou are killed, normally providing more meat than can be immediately consumed. This has been called sheer blood-lust – a piece of anthropomorphism, no doubt. But the wolf's overkill is really an evolutionary response to the same conditions that Jack had been talking about ever since Ottawa: when famine is close, it is wise to gorge to the limit if you can.

Seen panoramically, and in the sunshine of its brief summer, the wide, flat landscape of the Barren Ground presents a deceptively lush and gentle appearance. It is honeycombed with lakes and clothed in deep-green, low-growing vegetation between which birds and butterflies flit. Reflecting the vivid blue sky, the waters are alive with fish and waterfowl, while lying across the land like sleepy white snakes are the eskers. In the sides of these long, sandy ridges – formed by the sediment of sub-glacial ice-age riverbeds – foxes, wolves and wolverines excavate their dens.

But sunny days are never dependable. In a few minutes, under a furious blast of refrigerated wind and rain, the sky darkens. Then the muskeg is transformed into mush, and normally navigable rivers into torrents. Jack's party was overtaken time and again by these conditions, and was forced to wait them out in camp because of the danger to the heavily laden canoe. But even camping had suddenly become much more laborious than before. Wet moss made for poor kindling, and in 'the stickless land' the hunt for cooking fuel and brushwood to make smudges became far-ranging.

Meanwhile, they were on the alert for game and, as July turned to August, Jack told Edgar and Harold to watch for the southward migration of the caribou. On or about 4 August, it hit them. They were on Deville Lake when the animals broke the northern horizon and came skidding down the shallow, rocky scree towards the lake. Behind these pioneers came the main body of caribou, a vast herd of thousands, up to half a mile wide. The noise as they bore down on the water rose in a crescendo: cows bellowing to their bleating calves, the massed hooves rattling, the antlers clashing together as the beasts jostled for room. On arrival at the water's edge they plunged in and struck out for the farther shore. There was no going round. The caribou run is an expression of driven instinct, pressing forward in a straight line, whatever the obstacle: a river of meat which can take days to flow past.

When Jack, with Critchell-Bullock, saw the caribou come to the Thelon on 23 July 1925, he estimated that 10,000 beasts had crossed the river in two days. Critchell-Bullock put the number even higher. He also noted that, while the bulls were already getting their winter coats, the cows were in moult. As they entered the water the long hairs would detach in sheaves and eventually wash ashore. One of the Barren

Ground's most surprising sights after the autumn migration is the caribou hair piled thick as meadow hay along the riverbanks for hundreds of miles.

Deville Lake, where Edgar first saw this sight, lies thirty-five miles above the Ptarmigan Lake cairn, and is one of only two camping stages in the trip whose dates can be fixed. For here, Jack left a note in a cairn, intended for any trappers who happened along:

About Aug. 5th. Owing to bad weather and laziness travelling slowly. One big migration of caribou passed yesterday. Hope to see you all soon. J.H.

The bad weather was to be expected and the caribou migration made an excuse for some delay. But 'laziness' may be a veiled criticism of the stamina of Jack's two companions. He, of course, prided himself in his relentless energy and he may have become impatient with the younger men's inability to live with his pace. On the other hand, Jack himself could be subject to fits of indecisiveness when his restlessness led him in circles rather than a single direction. From Deville Lake, there were only five upstream miles to go before they reached the bifurcation of the Hanbury River. This was the 'summit' of the journey, for here the water, flowing northward from Smart Lake, divides into two rivers travelling in opposite directions – one the arm they had just canoed up, the other sweeping eastward down to join the Thelon. So from this point, for the first time since leaving Slave River, they were paddling with the stream.

At first it was easy going, but this did not last. On 12

August, above Sifton Lake, Harold began a letter to his family, the second dated evidence of the passage between Deville Lake and the winter cabin on the Thelon. The letter, which took three years to reach the Adlards in England, has survived only in part through a newspaper report.

It is now over one month since Hornby, Christian and I have seen a human being besides ourselves. That was on the Great Slave Lake at the end of July [*sic*]. We are now held up and have been for more than ten days, by storms and rain &c. and are unable to run the rapids into Sifton Lake, which is now very rough. A canoe would swamp at once.

Travelling has been slow because we have quite a load – about 500 pounds of flour, 1,500 rounds of .303 ammunition, three rifles, axes, stoves, tent, camera &c., 100 pounds of sugar, clothing, traps, tea, blankets, caribou meat, hides, candles and heaven knows what – about one ton in all, plus three men, all jammed into a twenty foot canoe. All this joint has to be packed on one's back from one small lake to another, and round rapids and falls which are absolutely impossible to run.

The country is called the Barren Land and it is rightly so-called. Nothing grows on the ground, or, rather, rocks but moss and sand, not a particle of wood for hundreds of miles, no human habitation for hundreds of miles, but game in the form of a caribou (reindeer), wolves, fox, hares, geese, ptarmigan &c. abounds. For a month now I have lived on caribou and tea and like it.

This letter is being written in the hopes of giving it to Blanchet, the government surveyor, whom we expect to meet homeward bound soon. He has been doing a quick trip of exploration up the various pieces of water up to the headwaters of the Thelon River, then to the junction of the Thelon and the Flanbury [*sic*] River and go back the way we have come. You should get this at Christmas, so cheerio. We started on the 25th of May at Edmonton and have paddled our canoe from Fort McMurray to Chipewyan, from there to Fort Smith, from Slave to Resolution on the Great Slave Lake and from there along Artillery Lake to present location. We intend staying for two winters and catch[ing] fur (at least Hornby is the licensed trapper), take photographs &c. and watch the animals go by. We live on our rifles and see nobody.

Winter quarter is an oasis of timber in the Barren Lands, and stretches for a hundred miles or more. We come out by way of Thelon River, Baker Lake, Chesterfield Inlet into Hudson Bay to Neilson. Tyrrell went through in 1900. About a dozen men all told have been through so far. Hornby went three years ago [*sic*] and the country is quite unexplored. If you don't hear within three years make enquiries from the Royal North-west Police.

Harold's dating needs to be treated with caution. As already noted, 'July' must have been accidentally substituted for 'June'. His statement that they had been held up 'for more than ten days' cannot mean that they had made no progress at all, since they had been at Deville Lake just a week earlier. His tendency to exaggerate comes through in his statement that 'nothing grows on this ground', as does his emphasis on the more romantic, even foolhardy, aspects of the expedition and his claim that they would be 'staying for two winters' in the Barrens. With their equipment, a two-winter residence was an almost suicidal idea.

At the same time, the letter contains much information about the state of the expedition at a critical moment. It confirms that Jack and company had been plagued by recent bad weather and forced to camp ashore to avoid losing their outfit in the river. It also gives a rough estimate of the size of that outfit, whose additions of meat and hides proves that there had been some successful hunting. It is clear, however, that their shooting was not a matter of picking off a caribou here and there according to need. Harold indicates that they had so far got through 500 rounds of .303 ammunition, a quarter of the total. Even allowing for approximation, this is extremely profligate, as if they had been blazing away. The original stock of ammunition had not been generous – in 1901, Hanbury had taken 3,000 rounds in addition to shotgun cartridges – and Jack's remaining 1,500 shells would have to be eked out for a further year. With limited space in the canoe, they could only carry away a fraction of the meat they killed. Behaving very like a wolf pack, they left much of it behind.

Harold's letter tells us also that Jack, just as he had earlier hoped to join up with the Stewarts, was now looking out for Guy Blanchet. Again there is the suspicion of unease in this, a hint that Jack would not mind spreading the responsibility for his two greenhorns. From the evidence of Harold's letter, Jack believed that Blanchet would be crossing from the Dubawnt River to the headwaters of the Thelon, descending that river as far as the Hanbury and going out by Reliance with – it was to be hoped – their letters. To take this route from Chipewyan to Reliance would not be a 'quick trip', however, nor an easy one, and to complete it within a June-to-August time-frame would have been a remarkable achievement, particularly as the Thelon headwaters had not been explored (by white men) before. On the other hand, if Blanchet had indeed gone that way, there would have been a high probability of meeting Jack, assuming Jack did not travel so fast as to pass the Thelon-Hanbury junction before Blanchet himself arrived there.

It did not happen, because Blanchet never went to the Thelon at all and never intended to. So how did Jack get hold of the idea? In their conference at Chipewyan on 1 or 2 June, Jack had turned down Blanchet's offer to accommodate him and Edgar, if they would jettison Harold. Did Blanchet follow up by encouraging Jack to believe they would all meet up anyway along the Hanbury? If so, he may later have felt guilty about this, though perhaps he convinced himself that Jack's party would in reality get no further than a winter camp beside Artillery Lake, making his deception harmless. In later life, Blanchet became a leading (if affectionate) critic of Jack's legend. But was he covering up a strained conscience?

Finally, this letter gives a rare clue to Harold's state of mind. He shows himself rather more anxious to impress his parents than to reassure them. The announcement that he lives exclusively 'on caribou and tea and like it' may be a defiant rejoinder to his father's accusations about liquor. Certainly his final suggestion that they contact the police 'if you don't hear within three years' is a chilling suggestion that he already knew the danger he was going into – and didn't care.

As soon as the weather allowed, Jack shot the rapids and took the canoe into Sifton Lake, which occupies a long bend in the undulating course of the Hanbury. Ahead of them was what Critchell-Bullock had called a 'treacherous stream', in which a fast but navigable current could turn into a dangerous rapid if the water level rose, as it would after a melt of snow or heavy rain. In some of the gorges, lined with steep cliffs, a canoe could be lightened and 'lined' down the river by men from the shore. In others, it had to be lifted out and carried. Danger was ever present in such stretches as Helen Falls and Dickson Canyon and the three were perhaps lucky that there was only one injury serious enough to delay them. Years later, H. Milton Martin, the Public Administrator of the North-West Territories, wrote that he had seen in 'a report of the hazards of the expedition whilst travelling from Fort Reliance to the Thelon River . . . that Jack Hornby hurt his back carrying an excess load on one of the portages'. With Jack incapacitated, progress through the portages would certainly have been slowed if it was not stopped altogether.

Another reminder of a different sort of danger came at Hanbury Lake, at the end of one of these portages. Just where they dropped their packs at the shore of the lake was a cairn and wooden post, carved with the words 'Lake

Hanbury. Named 13th August 1911, R. V. Radford, T. G. Street.' Street and Radford, whom Jack probably knew personally, were adventurers who had come down the Hanbury-Thelon from Reliance in search of musk-oxen. They had later left the Thelon at Schulz Lake, and headed for the Arctic coast, where they were both murdered after Radford struck an Eskimo guide.

The Radford and Street debacle was strikingly similar to the deaths of the two Oblate Fathers, Jean-Baptiste Rouvière and Guillaume LeRoux, whom Jack had guided on their way to convert the Eskimo at Coronation Gulf. Jack became a particular friend of Rouvière at Dease Bay on Great Bear Lake and travelled and hunted with him. The Eskimo knew Jack as 'the Little Father' – a reference to his short stature next to the tall priests – but also called him Hornybeena or Isumitak, which means 'the Thinker'. It was Jack's only experience of the Eskimo and seems to have been happy enough, although on one occasion he believed he had caught a man stealing from him. The alleged thief, Sinisiak, denying all, threatened to kill his accuser.

Jack was in the trenches when he heard from George Douglas that the two missionaries had disappeared. He replied:

I think I would be the best person to look for Father Rouvier[e] & Father Leroux. I would hardly think that the Esquimaux would kill them unless they had done something to make them afraid. Father Rouvier[e] was not the kind to do so but Father Leroux was a little too quick-tempered & not accustomed to handle savages.

But by the time he returned from France, it was known that the Fathers had been knifed and shot by two men, one being the same Sinisiak who'd previously threatened Jack. Their deaths had been a near replica of Radford's and Street's. Out on the trail, LeRoux had shouted at their native guides, although he did not actually strike one. Eskimo are not normally aggressive people, but Sinisiak and his accomplice were clearly exceptions and they exacted their revenge.

Just before the junction with the Thelon, the Hanbury passes through what Critchell-Bullock calls

> the most beautiful piece of country between Artillery Lake and the sea, that is, about Hawk Rock. There is exceptionally good fishing and although the scenery is not awe-inspiring as the Dickson Canyon may be, it is park-like, and dainty. It is the one spot in the river system travelled by us that I should like to return to.

After this they canoed on down the Thelon River, where, at last, they could make up time. There were no more rapids, no portages. In places the river spread to a width of more than a hundred yards and was only a few feet deep, above a shingle bottom. Elsewhere the water ran narrower, deeper and swifter through sandstone or granite gorges. Further downstream, around Grassy Island, the canoeists were refreshed to be back amongst trees again. Some were as tall and numerous as in the forested land – a riverbank growth that marked the beginning of the Thelon oasis.

Grassy Island was a large area, formed by a division in

the watercourse several miles long, and it contained one of the great sights of the Thelon: musk-oxen. Like the caribou, this creature has survived without further evolution from prehistory. In Europe, Pleistocene Age fossils have been found of it as far south as Austria, alongside the mammoth and the woolly rhinoceros. As the Ice Age receded, the musk-ox proved the most durable of these three great beasts, retreating to the cold plains of North America where its only serious predators were men with spears. Here it thrived until the coming of the carbine.

Massive in size and gently ruminant by nature, the musk-ox collects in small herds, generally from four to about twenty individuals. Critchell-Bullock had photographed the noble creature in 1925, and was 'struck by the cleanliness of their range. Although it was evident that several of the bulls we saw had occupied certain stamping grounds for some considerable time, there was no sign of dung anywhere.' The musk-oxen appealed strongly to the military man's 'aesthetic sense'. Burly horns fit their heads and curl down beside their faces exactly like a Napoleonic hat. The hair grows long, almost brushing the ground to form 'long black robes swinging like kilts'. The eyes are small, wide-set and watchful.

In behaviour, too, musk-oxen are appealingly unusual. Deeply attached to their stamping grounds, they never run far and move only when the food supply becomes scarce. The bulls patrol their borders (says Critchell-Bullock) 'like policemen on their beats', and, in rut, engage in violent skull-butting fights with their rivals, like pairs of elephantine rams. The bulls stand for a moment with their foreheads touching. Then they shuffle rapidly backwards to a distance of about twelve yards and hurl themselves forward again, their skulls meeting with an explosive crack. They go on doing this until one is battered into submission.

The musk-ox is normally slow to anger, although capable of a fiercesome bellow. If seriously threatened by a predator – for example, a wolf-pack – the bulls of the herd invariably stand at bay, in a tight, defensive formation around their cows and calves. If the attack is pressed, they will execute a sudden concerted charge and put the wolves to flight.

This refusal to run away has also been their tragedy. The coming of the rifle soon resulted in wholesale massacres in which, using dogs to hold a herd at bay, the natives would shoot into the defensive wall until the last animal had fallen. As sport, such slaughter soon palled. Big-game hunters like Warburton Pike grew ashamed to take advantage, but such finer feelings were confined to a few. With succulent flesh and a huge and valuable pelt, the musk-ox was enthusiastically hunted wherever its habitat could conveniently be reached. Tyrrell, at Chesterfield Inlet, noted musk-ox hides 'stacked by the Eskimo like haycocks' along the shore, awaiting sale. The musk-ox became a protected species in 1917, but by this time it was so scarce that the spot where Jack, Edgar and Harold now stood had become one of its last refuges. Not only had the island plenty of the marginal willow that was the musk-ox's favourite eating, but it was in an area devoid of humanity for hundreds of miles.

Just two days from here lay their winter camp. With the hold-ups along the Hanbury, it had taken most of July and August to negotiate a journey of a little less than two hundred miles from Reliance – no better than Jack had laboriously managed the previous year with Critchell-Bullock and significantly worse than was possible. The same journey, in the same season, was completed by Hanbury in 1901, H. S Wilson in 1928 and Inspector Trundle of the RCMP in 1929 – each in about three weeks. The combined effects of weather, injury, hunting, laziness and dawdling in the hope of meeting the Stewarts or Blanchet had slowed Jack up. He had perhaps a fortnight or three weeks at his disposal before the first snows came. There was much to do.

11. Log Cabin

From Grassy Island, the Thelon flows past increasingly tree-clad banks in a straight north-easterly direction for fifty miles, interrupted only by a sweeping S-bend about halfway along the reach. Here the oasis is at its thickest, with forest extending up to half a mile on each side of the stream. When Jack had camped here with Critchell-Bullock, close to the second bend which is now known as Hornby Point, he had exclaimed at the excellent spruce cover it afforded, the trees large enough to make logs for the construction of a cabin, the area extensive enough for one to expect that caribou would be wintering there. This was in late July 1925 and the place was captivating. A brook tumbled through the timber down a narrow creek, its steep, damp banks supporting patches of red raspberry, white flowering currant and columbine, though this was well north of the accepted range of such plants. Butterflies dodged between the willows that grew thickly along the riverbank. Fish broke the surface of the stream, and, at night, hooting owls floated from tree to tree.

Jack had immediately made a mental note of this as an ideal place in which to overwinter. Critchell-Bullock's diary makes no mention of it, although he later stated they had marked the spot on his map as a suitable one for building. There does not seem to have been time for a close examination of the forest, and they did not look for evidence of year-round game in the vicinity. However, cut tree stumps, between twenty and thirty years old, were seen, showing that at least one earlier party had camped, if not built there – almost certainly J. W. Tyrrell.

Jack's arrival with Edgar and Harold was probably on about 5 September – more than a month later than in the previous year. The summer had already guttered out. The weather was significantly colder and wetter, the north wind carrying with it the first snow. Yet the original promise of the place seemed undiminished as they beached the canoe and began looking for the south-facing terrace where Jack had seen Tyrrell's cuttings. They found it about thirty yards up the willow-fringed bank, and overlooking a wide sweep of the river which, at this point, was several hundred yards across. It was here they decided to build.

To construct a log house in the Barren Ground was no trivial challenge. The largest and most solid three-man cabin Jack had ever seen put up single-handedly was by the sea captain Lionel Douglas at Hodgson's Point in 1911. While his brother George and a third man were away on an extended reconnaissance of the Barren Ground, Captain Douglas built and furnished, entirely by his own craftsmanship and ingenuity, an impressive building – a mansion by comparison with most others of its type. Cabins were generally as niggardly as possible in size. Jack's one-man Fort Hornby at Reliance had been a mere six foot by eight, and a two-man dwelling was typically no more than fourteen by twelve. But although quicker to build and easier to keep warm, these confined spaces had very particular problems of their own. Sitting out winter storms, perhaps for weeks at a time, men were easily prey to the psychological condition popularly known as 'cabin fever'. It was to obviate any such problems that Captain Douglas had built so generously at Hodgson's Point. But here, on the Thelon, Jack could not afford the kind of luxury that he was, in any case, temperamentally opposed to.

So he took the plan of the standard two-man log cabin and added two feet to the side walls to make a building fourteen foot square, just big enough for three bunks. He chose a sloping site so that, when the floor was levelled, a vertical bank of earth formed the whole of the cabin's rear wall – a sensible detail which conserved time and timber and provided extra protection from the prevailing conditions. Logs for the front and side walls were between eight and eighteen inches in diameter, obtained by the felling of a dozen spruces or more. The tree trunks were cut to length, again by axe, since there was no saw in the outfit. These were laid in careful sequence, a single log going down first to begin the front wall, followed by the first logs of the two side walls, their ends deeply notched with an axe to form a rough but firm corner joint. The second logs of the front wall – now divided to make room for a centrally placed door – were laid next, and so on until a height of about five feet was reached. Roofing spars were laid from the sides to two ridge poles extending forward above the door to provide a porch canopy. The roof had a shallow pitch which was covered with spruce branches, earth and shingle fetched from the riverbank. Meanwhile, off-cuts from the felled spruce were used for a second building, a small storehouse beside the cabin. In this they kept the canoe's fittings, as well as tools, ammunition, fuel and food.

In each outside wall of the main cabin was a small opening for a window, twelve inches square and filled with one of the precious panes of glass safely, if precariously, transported from Edmonton – or possibly only from Reliance, where they may have been obtained from the cache at Fort Hornby. The cabin's rear (mud) wall was revetted with spruce brush and reindeer moss, and gaps were plugged everywhere with river mud as well as moss. The cabin door was made from slats which Jack must have brought with him, also perhaps from Reliance. The McClary stove, set up near the centre of the room, was connected to the chimney-pipe which rose through a hole in the roof. Three bunks were constructed, one in the north-east corner for Jack and the other two on the west side for Edgar and Harold. They also made a rough table, set against the earth wall on the north side. The rest of the furniture comprised their trunks and suitcases.

While building, they lived in the tent, pitched next to the site. Construction went slowly. The period of almost two months it took to complete the shack was partly attributable to the difficulty of working with a limited selection of tools and on frozen ground. But the most important delaying factor was their increasingly urgent preoccupation with laying in stocks of fresh meat.

A parable is told by the Chipewyans about food and survival. The whisky-jack and the ground squirrel were quarrelling, as usual. The thrifty squirrel, a good hunter, thought it prudent to go hungry and to lay aside as much food as possible for the long winter. But the whisky-jack, too lazy to hunt, would always fly after the squirrel, to see where he hid his stores, returning later to root out the carefully cached food and stuff himself to bursting. At last, exhausted by trying to outwit the whisky-jack, the squirrel confronted him, protesting stridently that every creature must hunt and cache for himself. Just as loudly, the whisky-jack retorted that food was free for all and, if he didn't like it, the squirrel should eat all his food in one meal and forget about caching it. The argument shrilled across the land until the Great Spirit grew tired of listening. To teach the quarrelsome pair a lesson he took away their memories, so that both creatures forgot the whereabouts of the hidden food. And, to this day, these two are despised in the Barren Ground for always going hungry, always scavenging and always making a nuisance of themselves.

Beneath the proto-Christian moral about dealing honestly and sharing the fruits of the earth, this fable expresses the essential dilemma of survival in the North. From the Indian perspective, both the squirrel and the whisky-jack are in a measure right, although their methods conflict. When there is plenty, it is obvious that you should eat well and also cache meat, frozen and out of predators' reach, for later retrieval. But the important point, extremely relevant to Jack and his companions, is that, in times of shortage, skilful day-by-day hunting and the husbanding of what is caught become a matter of prime concern. Jack was still, at this stage, making confident noises about his ability in both these disciplines.

When in the North, his conversation revolved a great deal around the caribou, a food source available to the Barren

Ground hunter at certain times not only in prime quality but in practically unlimited quantity. However, the migration patterns of the caribou – what makes them move when they do, and why they go where they go – have always seemed mysterious, even mystical. The Indians said, 'Like ghosts, they come from nowhere. They fill up the land. They vanish.' And a Chipewyan proverb has it that 'Nobody knows the ways of the wind and the caribou.' But Jack honestly believed he did know them. He regarded the life cycle of the caribou, its mating habits and migrations, as an open book. His Caribou Report might be called a transcription of that book.

It is said that the migrations of the caribou are very irregular but I found they would be as regular as the seasons if their courses were not deflected by the Indians and Eskimo or on account of the sea or large lakes not being frozen over or the country having been burnt . . .

It is about the first week in August that the Indians move up to the barren lands to meet the [female] caribou as they make their first movement southwards. The caribou have now almost shed all their old hair and their skins are beginning to get good but . . . it is not before the end of the month that they begin to get fat. During this time caribou could be seen moving for several days in small bands of ten to several hundreds. During the summer there were always bull caribou to be seen along the barren points of the lake [Artillery Lake] and also on the high ridges and also on the islands close to Hunter's Bay where they could get some respite from the flies . . . The caribou are in the fattest condition from towards the end of September until the first week in October. About the beginning of October, during the first real cold spell, the mating season commences. The caribou now congregate in countless herds at the edge of the woods of the barrens, all the bull caribou having come out of the woods.

According to this version, then, the caribou in the Barren Ground were at their most nutritious at the end of September and early October – at just the time Jack had arrived with Edgar and Harold at Hornby Point. Prime caribou, weighing up to 300 lb, then carried as much as 25 lb of fat on their backs alone. These are Jack's figures from his Caribou Report of 1925, and they mean that the food value of a single animal might amount to 80–100 lb of meat and 60 lb of offal. If an active man in the Barren Ground needs around ten pounds of fresh, fat meat a day, then a single caribou of this quality would probably be consumed by three such men in four to five days; over an eight-month winter, a store of at least fifty of these prime carcasses should therefore be caught, frozen and cached. More would be required if the beasts were smaller or carried a lower ratio of fat to lean flesh.

Jack's report suggests that, with a proper understanding of caribou migration, such a target of kills was achievable, since the herds were easy enough to find. However, the killing had to be done in a very short hunting season – three or at most four weeks – because the quality of the meat soon deteriorated 'on the hoof'.

Towards the end of October and the beginning of November the bull caribou come [back] into the woods singly and in small herds from two to twenty. At this time they are poor and not at all good eating. In November – the old bulls cast their horns. Towards the end of November most caribou move southwards, by many circles, back into the barren lands, especially the females and the young, and again in December large bands of caribou are moving southwards into the woods, females and young ones remaining outside the woods during the whole winter in large numbers but most of the bulls go[ing] into the woods. During the very stormy weather the caribou leave the woods and go on to large lakes, into open places, because when the winds are strong the caribou cannot detect any strange sounds and so are scared. In winter the caribou . . . penetrate far into the woods but do not always frequent the same locality . . . In April the female caribou move out of the woods and by May there are no female caribou to be seen in the woods.

The views expressed here, and the confidence behind them, determined more than anything else the timing of Jack's arrival at Hornby Point. But it is important to stress that the calculation did not depend on their meeting a large-scale caribou migration. In Jack's view, all that mattered for the white man overwintering in the Barren Ground was to be on the fringe of the woods between September and mid-October, just before and during rutting, when large numbers of animals assembled and were in prime condition. All this was unequivocally based on the assumption that the woods around this long river bend were an isolated winter range for significant numbers of caribou, and that all he had said in his report about the behaviour of the herds, drawing on his observations close to the main treeline at Artillery Lake two hundred miles to the south-west, also held good for this oasis. If it did, all was well and his target bag of fifty plus caribou in three weeks, though not easy, was at least realistic.

But what if it didn't? What if the caribou migrated straight past the Thelon oasis and thundered on upstream to winter in the deep forests on either side of Great Slave Lake? In these circumstances, two conditions would determine the hunter's success: timing and distance. If he was in place in time for the migration, he could hope to kill most of the caribou he needed by slaughtering them *en masse* as they came through. Failing that, he had to be able to range far and wide across the Barrens, in search of those smaller breeding herds of between two and twenty cows, each attached to a single bull. This meat would be very good but, once killed, it would need to be run quickly and safely to base from twenty, thirty or even forty miles away. This could only be done with dogs and sleds.

As it happened, Jack, Edgar and Harold, beginning their Thelon winter, could fulfil neither of these alternative conditions. Firstly, if there *had* been a large migration into or through this part of the Thelon oasis, they had palpably missed it. Secondly, they had no dogs. This second fact calls for further explanation.

Jack must have decided early on to make this an expedition without dogs, though it was a surprising decision, contrary to the conventional wisdom. Trappers, who always wintered in or close to the Barrens because winter was the season of the finest white fur, invariably had dogs with them. Indians also always took dogs when travelling in winter in the Barrens and Jack himself, on previous Barren Ground trips, had done so. Why, on this occasion, did he not take any?

Jack had never, as it happened, thought dogs were indispensable and, for environmental as well as economic reasons, he frequently deplored the canine population explosion that, as he claimed, had occurred in the North in recent years. In his Caribou Report he wrote of the 'ever increasing number of dogs kept by the natives [which] ever tend to the great destruction of animals [i.e. caribou]'. In addition, he believed (and more to the point here) that these numerous dogs 'materially assist the Indians to be in a perpetual state of want' because they ate more meat or fish (5–6 lb each day) than the extra food they brought in. The search for enough dog food was a wilderness dweller's major and continuing preoccupation but, at the same time, that extra effort was a price which often had to be paid. Without dogs, no distance in the North could be travelled overland if there were loads to carry. Jack, the distance-walker, the expert self-starver, had begun to regard himself as an exception to this rule. By 1921, he was writing to George Douglas during his second solitary year at Fort Hornby:

> This year I have no dogs, which at last I have found to be a big source of expense & also the cause of keeping me on the move.

Yet Jack, like any trapper, had been fond of dogs as companions. The abuse they received at the hands of their Indian owners in summer appalled him, and they suffered in winter too. At Fort Hornby in 1920–21, he was sometimes even more distressed at the dogs' plight than at his own starving condition. Too often, Barren Land dogs died or were killed from back-breaking winter work and malnutrition.

In 1924, Jack and Critchell-Bullock had set out with six dogs – Skinny, Rowdy, Porky, Jack, Bhaie and Whitey – which, since they were to travel some of the way with a heavy outfit across snow and ice, was essential. Despite the best intentions of their two mushers, both at heart equally humane men, the team could not avoid suffering and ultimate destruction. Occasionally a dog fell victim to a man's irrational temper – a variant of 'cabin fever' – as when Critchell-Bullock became so infuriated with (the dog) Jack, for continually barking at wolves in the dark, that he knocked him cold and thought he had killed him. At other times, dogs refused to go forward, or ran off after caribou, or fought amongst themselves, and would be painfully whipped. And if food was short they starved. When Critchell-Bullock's favourite, Bhaie (the name he gave the dog means 'friend' in Hindustani), was rendered useless by a suppurating paw, Jack turned away in distress as his partner put a bullet through the dog's head. The demise of Whitey, the last remaining dog of the six, affected him even more. An individual of this name had been with Jack at Fort Hornby in 1920–21 and was the only one to survive with him. On this occasion he had written in his diary, presumably with Whitey in mind, 'I could never eat a dog. When I am starving, my dogs are starving also.' Perhaps this Whitey was the same individual – a large dog and a sterling worker who could carry a pack fifty pounds in weight, and to whom Critchell-Bullock paid tribute as 'one of the most faithful dogs I have known'. Whitey became the canine hero of Malcolm Waldron's *Snow Man: John Hornby in the Barren Ground* and his death is written as an emotional set-piece in which Critchell-Bullock reluctantly agrees to shoot Whitey on Jack's behalf, then watches Jack give the worn-out dog, as a last supper, their only remaining slab of edible caribou meat. While Whitey, with his decayed teeth, pathetically mumbles at this, Jack plays out a charade of pretending to pick up his gun for some quite different purpose before giving it to Critchell-Bullock. But as he walks past the dog, he suddenly realizes that only he can shoot Whitey and whirls round and fires in one movement, killing the dog instantly. With the echo of the shot still resounding in his ears, Critchell-Bullock realizes that it had to be that way. Hornby would never have forgiven another man for killing his beloved Whitey.

So, partly out of compassion, and partly because he considered them a possible extra liability, Jack had made a conscious decision to do without dogs in 1926. And, as he settled with Edgar and Harold into their winter base, the lack of a dog team was not seen as an issue. It is never mentioned in the diary which Edgar would shortly resume writing, and there is no other evidence that Jack regretted it.

Indeed, from his point of view, there was still nothing to be very nervous about. While he had admittedly missed the caribou migration, Jack still believed that caribou rutted near the woods of the oasis before coming into the trees themselves for the winter – precisely the notion which Guy Blanchet had warned him against during their conversations at Fort Chipewyan and which was still to be tested. But, even if Blanchet was right and there were no caribou, Jack still had an alternative which he must have thought fail-safe. Most subsequent discussion of the difficulties which Jack had in feeding his party has centred on the inadequacies of ptarmigan and river fish as a back-up diet, or on the absence in these woods of the snowshoe rabbit. Only Critchell-Bullock appears to have appreciated Jack's true calculation. Commenting after the publication of Edgar's diary, he wrote:

> There is no doubt in my mind that Hornby visualized the prospect of caribou failing to frequent his camp-site throughout the winter, and that he intended in this event to shoot ovibus (musk-oxen).

Musk-oxen were, of course, protected from hunters by law, but their killing was allowed when human life was at risk. Jack had seen musk-oxen in these very woods the previous year with Critchell-Bullock. He had watched them twenty-five miles upstream *this* year. Moreover, he did not consider that they ever migrated. In short, these massive, inquisitive, home-loving animals, so pathetically amenable to death by rifle fire, would provide an easy source of emergency meat if, at any stage, his group found themselves *in extremis*.

It was all, of course, a mistake. And from this mistake, from the blindness of its certainty, Jack's final tragedy would flow.

12. Wind Chill

For the past six weeks, Edgar had driven himself hard. He worked on the cabin with axe and spade. He learned how to set trap-lines with Jack, and how to identify animal tracks in the snow. He helped Harold fish in the still-unfrozen river and tramped the woods and the Barren Ground in search of game, his rifle slung carelessly from the crook of his arm.

From the start, he had much preferred this last activity to labouring. When the wind was not too strong, and the clouds not too louring, it felt good to be a hunter in the snow, padding across the frozen crust in snowshoes, listening to sounds behind the wind, scenting the air. But increasingly it had been less fun. For days at a time there was nothing but blizzard, when the gale turned into a malevolent bully, pounding his face, freezing his eyeballs, buffeting him until he staggered. At such times it was almost impossible to travel any distance. And meanwhile, as winter steadily encroached, the tent at night seemed dirty, cluttered and chilled, though, as yet, the thermometer still kept well above 0°F (−17°C). Edgar lay on his bed of knobbly brushwood, wrapped in his red Hudson's Bay blankets, trembling furiously for the few moments before sleep blacked everything out. At such times he longed for the cabin to be finished, for the stove to be fired up to blazing redness, for order to be re-established, for a proper bunk to call his own. Then he resolved to work harder than ever on the house.

There had, with all this, been little opportunity or energy for journal writing. Yet from time to time he would secretly unfold his letters from home and read them through. It was only at such moments of indulgence that Edgar really felt homesick. So familiar from the weekly letters Colonel Christian had sent him at school, his father's neat, disciplined handwriting dragged at his heart.

> Just a few lines to say good-bye & to wish you, with all my heart, all success in your great adventure . . . Try to keep a sort of diary of your life till you come back, even if you only make very short entries once a week or so.

At this point, remembering the sole diary entry he had so far managed, his conscience prodded him. For a while, he considered waiting until they moved into the cabin. But now, on 14 October, he changed his mind. Yesterday they'd killed a caribou on the Barren Ground and feasted. Today had been warmer and, while the thaw ruled out hunting, it allowed good progress on the building. Edgar felt in such a positive frame of mind that he pulled out one of the notebooks entitled *Records* and, sitting in the tent by candlelight, made his first entry for four months.

> October 14th '26. Weather turned much milder and made travelling on shoes bad so could not get in rest of meat. I took a short walk down stream in morning

but saw no tracks beside weasel. All spent rest of day digging out sand from the house and fixing up the roof permanently. Temp. 26 F. wind moderate. north Easterly.

For the next sixteen days, he kept a daily record of fluctuating winds and temperatures, of hunting, trapping, skinning, photography and home improvement. For a while, the fierce wind abated and, with the snow again freezing, they could go further abroad. Jack and Harold packed in the rest of the meat, piling it in the storehouse, while Edgar saw to the traps. But after a few days the wind returned, at times confining them to the camp so that 'being in all day was like Sunday in civilization'. Harold and Jack constructed bunks for the house and began the porch. Edgar sewed moccasins, but whenever he could he ventured out to his traps. Thick, drifting snow buried the trap-lines, but Edgar stuck to his task for, as Jack told him, 'i pelt means i bannock'.

The art of trapping, according to Critchell-Bullock, was not practised in the same way by Indians, Eskimo and white men. The Eskimo trapped close to his base and exclusively used small fish – or larger fish chopped up – which had been allowed to putrefy before being placed on the trigger plate of a carefully placed spring-trap. If one of these was unavailable, he was expert at making deadfalls and snares. The Indian, by contrast, waited until he had made a sizeable caribou kill in the course of his winter wandering. Having removed the best meat for his own use, he would leave the carcasses on the ground, where they had fallen and been eviscerated, set his traps all around, and then move on. The fur-bearing animals would be caught either approaching the bait or coming away, and be harvested as and when the band returned to that location. Finally, there were the white trappers, who were both more systematic than the Indian and more far-ranging than the Eskimo. They were fond of talking up the mystique of their art, with many personal rituals and techniques. But, in essence, they were all guided by the same combination of experience and intuition.

Their preparations prior to the trapping season were rigorous. Starting from his cabin, the trapper plotted his trap-lines, no more than ten miles in length (unless there was an intermediate cabin), and blazed them with axe marks in the trees. Just before the streams froze over, the traps' sites themselves were chosen, usually about two hundred in all. It was important to find sites that would not become too deeply drifted up (something in which Jack had evidently been less than successful); with this proviso in mind, ideal locations included existing animal-runs, the crowns of hummocks or the bends of streams. Short anchor chains, each ending with a transverse toggle, were dug into the ground, marked with a willow stick and allowed to freeze in place. Meanwhile, the traps were carefully checked to see that their jaws, either with or without teeth and sprung by a central pressure plate, were in working order. They were coded by number, according to size and the prey appropriate to them:

  0 – squirrel, ermine
  1 – marten, mink, muskrat
  1½ & 2 – fox, hare

3 — wolverine, fox, lynx, beaver
4 — wolf
5 & 6 — bear

To remove the human scent, the traps were boiled in a broth containing various ingredients such as spruce needles, alder twigs and beeswax — every trapper had his own personal recipe. They were then hung from trees some distance from the camp and thereafter handled, if possible, only with hooks. As the season approached, they were taken down the line, attached one by one to the anchoring chains and sunk in snow-holes. Fox urine or the sexual organs of any small animal could be smeared on the traps, which were then baited with fish or offal and covered by a thin, specially cut disc of snowcrust poised just over the jaws. The crust was sprinkled with frozen blood and loose snow and the trap left to await its first victim. A dedicated trapper visited his lines every two or three days   an arduous journey unless he had a dog team and sled.

Most of this information is relayed in Critchell-Bullock's report, and can therefore be taken as the theory of trapping as Jack knew it, even if he did not always adhere to it himself. Critchell-Bullock devotes considerable space to the subject, but he himself found no pleasure in trapping, coming to believe it cruel. His response was perhaps typical of an Englishman of his background. Ultimately he saw the trapper, with his commercial motives, as the converse of the sportsman. The latter pits his wits against nature, developing an almost mystical respect for the animals he tries to kill. However, when a trapper thinks about his prey he is only 'considering profits, contemplating the future, and making quick returns'. It is not to minimize the suffering of his victims that he goes frequently to his trap-line, but merely because 'the trap that is holding an animal cannot catch another until that animal is removed'.

Edgar's trap-line ran down through the woods at a transverse angle from the cabin and consisted of number-one traps – a 'marten' line. A second line of traps numbered 1½ or 2, designed for foxes and hares, ran upstream and was in Harold's care, while a third line was laid on the Barrens high above the cabin. Edgar, who attended to his line assiduously, at least in the first part of the winter, was technically an illegal trapper. Only Jack held a licence and, in any case, the fox season did not begin until 15 November (lasting until 1 April). The infringement did not matter a great deal, as the amount of fur taken was minimal. In the next fortnight it amounted to three weasel, a marten, two whisky-jack, a white fox, some mice and, on 23 October, a wolverine. This last – also known as the carcajou – was not only an ugly-looking beast, about the size of a middling dog, it was a carrion-eater and scavenger, and so was universally regarded with contempt. Even its scientific title, *gulo luscus*, branded it a glutton. When they found this one, its legs gripped in the serrated jaws of the steel trap, 'struggling and snarling, the voracious brute', its subsequent death made them feel 'very satisfied'.

Edgar was keeping a young white fox. It must have sprung a number-one trap and been held in the jaws without suffering the usual broken bones. Later Jack found another live cub, 'a good companion', as Edgar writes, 'for our other little captive'. Fox was among the main interests of the Barren Ground trapper. Its pelt (when in prime condition) could fetch premium prices and it was not at all difficult to catch. Despite its reputation for cunning, the arctic fox, even as an adult, was often unafraid to come close to a man. Critchell-Bullock had once caught one simply by bending and picking it up with his bare hands. Edgar's pets were probably seen as charming curiosities, though he only once mentions them in his diary. Perhaps Jack had warned him against becoming too attached to the cubs, because they would surely have to be killed eventually. We do not even know if he gave them names.

The disappointing fur catch – not just of white fox but of marten and weasel too – was hardly going to 'make a fortune in furs for the boy', an expectation Jack had sometimes voiced on his way into the Thelon. But it was far more ominous for another reason. As Jack knew, the small carni-vores ran after the larger game, taking advantage of leftovers from wolf and Indian kills of caribou. In places where caribou collected, the numbers of these small fur-bearers overflowed. But wherever their food sources ran only to mice, lemmings and squirrels, they were sharply reduced. The infrequency of fox and marten made it unlikely that many wolf and caribou were concentrated in the area. Perhaps Blanchet had been right, and the oasis was not a winter caribou range. Jack could live with this disappointment, however, because he had two remaining hopes for a caribou supply.

The first of these was that the caribou might still be found higher up, on the tundra itself. Initially this had looked doubtful until, on 18 October:

Jack returned in the evening with glad news having seen 30 caribou on a distant ridge behind Camp, so tomorrow we all go out in last effort for Winter's grub.

But, on the next day:

We all started out early for to see if caribou were grazing still on ridge behind camp but were soon disappointed in seeing nothing for miles around.

In the caribou hunt, this cycle of expectation and disappointment was to be repeated many times during the winter. Spurred by that initial sighting of the herd, Jack built himself a windbreak, or lookout post, on a ridge which lay above the edge of the woods. Here, after a stiff climb through the trees and a slog of perhaps half a mile across open ground, he would station himself with his rifle cocked, scanning the great empty snowscape. For hours, almost motionless and apparently impervious to the bone-chilling cold, he occupied this post, squinting into the wind through snow goggles across the undulating blanket of snow, waiting for a black dot to move here, or an antler to break the white horizon there. Day after day he did this and saw nothing.

The second remaining possibility for getting caribou was one which required more elaborate preparation: to establish a remote secondary base from which they could extend their hunting ground beyond the ten-mile band of outland to which they were limited from the shack. It would mean building a secure cache where rations could be permanently stored and where killed meat could wait for later collection.

It was decided to make such a cache upstream, at a site that may have been chosen on their way down in September. The exact location of the cache and camping ground was unknown until Robert Common overwintered on the Thelon with five companions to mark the fiftieth anniversary of Jack's trip. Common found the site of the cache about sixteen miles upstream, on the Thelon's north bank, in a stand of trees and beside a tongue of pink boulders which extends into the river, pushed there by a riffle or shallow current fast-flowing over a shingle bed. There he saw:

> a little hollow where there were old axe cuts on some
> of the stumps. I was certain I had found the cache itself.
> I spent the night there and the shelter of the spot is
> probably the best for 30 km.

As this indicates, it was not a badly chosen spot. From here Jack could conduct a more wide-ranging hunt over the Barrens, on ground which the enigmatic caribou may find preferable and which was, in addition, much closer to the known haunts of the 'emergency' musk-oxen. Its distance from the cabin, measured along the riverbank, could be reduced to perhaps twelve miles if one left the shelter of the valley, cut the river bend and crossed the exposed Barren Ground. There was no cabin built there, but the cache would have been constructed on legs to keep it well clear of predators – a smaller version of the one Jack and Critchell-Bullock had put up at Fort Reliance. Here one of the tents would also have been left so that a hunter could spend two or three days at the place, bringing to it any meat killed and caching it there for subsequent packing, or man-hauling on a sled, back to the cabin.

At the beginning of November there comes a break in Edgar's diary lasting almost a month. This is not explained, but it perhaps signalled a period of settled weather in which the party was using up a great deal of energy out of doors. They were working flat out to finish the cabin, as well as fishing and trapping, and in the midst of it all celebrating Harold's twenty-seventh birthday on 14 November. They passed many cold days on caribou-watch up on the ridge and probably made several further expeditions to the upriver cache. It was during one of these hunting trips, as the storms returned to pin him down in the tent, that Edgar again picked up the thread of his diary.

> 21st November. Hunting. Storming all day on barrens so had to lay up all day which meant 1 day's less hunting owing to lack of grub.

> 22nd. About 8 a.m. wind dropped and made travelling possible. Walked up river on ridges till 12 AM then turned home. Tracks of Caribou going south in front of storm. On way home wind strong and very cold. Could not keep hands and face warm at all. Returned to shelter at dusk. 16 miles.

Edgar does not mention a companion on this trip. Was he by himself? It seems highly unlikely. Probably Jack was with him, while Harold remained at the cabin. In any case, these upriver expeditions lasted only three or four days. Next day, having once again failed to secure caribou meat, Edgar was on his way back to the cabin.

> 23rd. Started early to walk back to main shack. Only had Bannock to breakfast on. The wind very cold and fairly strong so forced to keep to river for shelter. A steady tramp all the way and bitter wind, getting home in 5 hours, 16 miles.

Having no thermometer with him at the upriver cache, Edgar did not record any temperatures there. But the deliberate avoidance of the Barren Ground on the return journey shows that an extra five or six miles walking along the riverbank was preferable to exposure to the worst weather, and it is clear that the thermometer had now sunk well below 0°F. The next reading Edgar records, two days later, is −15°F.

Simple temperature readings do not, of course, tell the whole story, because they omit the most important factor governing the winter conditions as they are experienced on the Thelon: wind. When fresh snow has fallen, any wind over ten m.p.h. will begin to lift ice particles off the ground and raise a bank of snow-mist, which, as it becomes more dense, will reduce visibility to a few yards. At the same time, wind causes the snow to drift, even under clear skies, creating a treacherous unevenness in the depth of snow underfoot. Finally, the wind pelts this ice-dust painfully into the face, an exhausting exposure if it lasts any length of time.

Wind chill is a yet more significant effect. Anyone exposed to wind is considerably colder than in shelter, because the stronger the wind, the quicker the body cools – which is the reason why Edgar 'could not keep hands and face warm at all' when hunting from the upriver cache. There are various methods of expressing wind chill, but its effect is illustrated by the fact that in completely still air, exposed skin does not freeze until below −50°F, whereas a fresh-to-strong twenty-five m.p.h. breeze will cause it to do so at a mere −15°. It was the fear of frostbite more than anything that prevented Jack, Edgar and Harold from travelling or working out of doors when the wind blew. Wind chill, not the thermometer reading, is what made the Barren Ground the most inhospitable place in North America.

Next day, back at the cabin, they at last enjoyed a meal – a 'fine big trout' hooked by Harold through the ice of the now-frozen Thelon. But it was obviously a great disappointment that the energy expended on hunting had yielded no caribou meat – and they had not even, as Jack must surely have lamented, sighted musk-oxen. That night, Edgar disconsolately summed up the hunting trip for his diary:

> We have now hunted over all country as marked [on Tyrrell's map] 'Musk ox numerous' but have seen none to get Photographic records of in winter scenes.

Edgar saw the lack of musk-oxen as a misfortune – a frustrated photographic ambition. But it meant something far more serious to Jack, who may never have told Edgar of his intention of killing musk-oxen if the caribou failed. That contingency had now occurred, and the fail-safe musk-oxen alternative, too, had begun to look a forlorn hope.

13. Famine

As the days grew shorter – the sun was only now above the horizon for a couple of hours – so did the food supply and Edgar's diary entries became preoccupied with efforts to find game close to the cabin.

25th. Temperature low all day and wind blowing. Jack set net in Willow for Ptarmigan in afternoon. I took a walk on to the Barrens but saw nothing although views good. Harold looked at Hook but no fish. −15°F.

26th November. All took it easy being cold all day and having no meat. Went with Jack to look at Ptarmigan net and we disturbed about 20 from close by but none in the net, a stroke of bad luck. Afterwards with Jack, reba[i]ted hook and line (no fish). Harold walked out on Barrens but saw nothing.

27th. A fine day but we are taking Life Easy to economize in grub. I went out to barrens and got 1 fox and reset trap. Jack dug up all the fish left, 60 in all, which will last just 2 weeks and then, if we have no meat we will be in a bad way.

From this entry until its last, except for two gaps, Edgar's daily record now continues unbroken as a story with a single theme: a chronicle of hunger and the obsessive search for food.

The motif of food colours all other preoccupations. Weather conditions limit hunting. An injury or illness is relevant according to whether or not the sufferer can hunt. Time spent repairing snowshoes or moccasins is so much time lost to the hunt. The recording of bird and animal life is a reminder of possible food. And, even when Harold tries resourcefully to make the long northern nights pass more cheerfully, Edgar's thoughts are elsewhere.

29th [November]. Harold made a pack of cards which will now help to pass the evening by, although I wish to goodness there was no time for cards.

On 2 December, on a calm, cold day, Jack and Harold set out on another four-day trip upriver. Edgar, who had perhaps been more of a liability than a help on previous forays, stayed behind, visiting nets and traps (fruitlessly) and laying floorboards in the house. Still alone as the thermometer sank to −37° F, he was fighting off despondency in the midst of these oddly silent woods.

The place seems very desolate and I feel certainly lonely by myself but can always find lots of odd jobs to do and keep busy to pass the time.

But tinkering was a cheerless occupation when Edgar wanted to be busy with the only thing that would prove him useful in Jack's eyes: obtaining food. When he could not fill the void with work, the problem of food recurred over and over. Edgar had been hungry before, of course. Children and young adults are willing to eat at any hour, but Edgar had been brought up in the kind of regime that strictly forbad eating between meals. Yet the hollow stomach of a Kent prep-school boy was an expression of healthy appetite rather than chronic privation. The dull hunger he now experienced, never satisfied by the bannock and bit of fish that were his daily ration, nagged at him with the inner voice of an addict craving his drug.

On the third day, as Edgar carried fuel into the cabin, a log slipped and

hit me plum[b] in middle of back laying me out for a time and keeping me indoors resting. The monotonous silence was broken during the day by a little flock of American white winged Crossbills coming around.

Jack and Harold returned on the evening of the third day, 4 December, exhausted from what had been another 'fruitless' journey. The following morning, Jack explained their awkward situation. The caribou had failed. The musk-oxen had failed. There were no wolves around and very few small mammals. The fishing was very difficult as the river ice thickened. The nets set for ptarmigan – the willow or rock grouse – did not seem to work. They were trying too hard and getting too little. They were in trouble.

Jack, in whatever terms he used, was describing the same kind of trouble that Scott had been in. Edgar had had this spelled out to him, with his fellow Dover College pupils, by

Commander Teddy Evans of the Scott expedition, a man who had known 'how to starve' as well as Jack. The message, at any rate, was clear. It was time for a change of strategy. There would be no more exhausting trips after big game. From now on, they would confine their efforts to trapping, hooking and netting whatever food they could in the vicinity of the camp. Edgar clearly articulates this on 5 December:

> Now we must throw up trapping and practically den up and get hold of any grub we can, without creating big appetite, by hunting on short cold days.

And, on 6 December, he conducted a food audit:

> On counting fish see there are enough for 14 days at 2 per day and then we have only 100 lbs flour between us till spring when Caribou ought to come again. 1 walked out on the Barrens and got 1 fox but it was damn thin and not even a meal for us. Harold got 1 Wolverine by Creek, so that's a good meal.

In fact, the fish lasted less than ten days. They were cooked in wolverine fat, which Jack had been careful to boil off and scrape out from every particle from the hide, muscles, inner organs and intestines of the animal caught on 6 December. The fat of the despised beast was a vital addition to the meals of scrawny birds, fish and small mammals which were now their only alternative to bannock. Edgar pays tribute to it in the diary on 16 December when, without any sign of regret, he reports that the two pet foxes had been finally killed and eaten.

Having no fish we had foxes for supper and they certainly seemed exceptionally good with a little bit of flour added and warmed up in Wolverine fat.

For a while the river had seemed the most promising food source, yielding four good-sized trout and a loach over the previous ten days. But when Jack decided to reinforce Harold's fishing line with nets set below the ice, he did not appreciate the strenuous ten days of cutting and maintaining ice holes that this would entail. On 4 December, Jack laboured on the thick ice until eight p.m. – that is, for several hours by moonlight. Finally, on 18 December the net was put in, anchored in the water between two ice holes by hammered-in stakes. At nightfall the net had already taken a decent trout, and they were full of hopes for the next day.

19th December. All anxiously waiting to see what was in the net by daybreak and to our disappointment when we got there the floats were frozen somewhere in the middle [of the refrozen ice]. All day we laboured in vain digging holes in the ice but were no further ahead by dark. 1 trout on hooks.

On 20 December, they finally succeeded in retrieving the net, which contained only 'one fat Jack fish'. But the net itself had become ripped to shreds during their efforts to free it, requiring two days of patient repair work by Jack. Yet, as

Edgar relayed, he thought this 'well worth the time spent if only a few fish get into it'.

A few fish did *not* get into it. The net was reset on Christmas Day and, for the next fortnight, it was visited daily, Jack laboriously hacking through the thick ice to get at the floats and net. But day by day he found nothing and by 8 January he had had enough. The net was never set again.

Meanwhile, Jack's attempts at netting ptarmigan were an even more humiliating failure. In fact, by setting the nets in the willow, he was bound to fail. The only way to net the bird in any quantity was to take it on the wing, exploiting its habit of skimming low over rising ground by setting long nets on the crest of a ridge. The alternative method of taking this relative of the Scottish grouse was to snare it on the ground. To do this, the Eskimo built fences of willow sticks in a funnel formation, with a snared gate where they narrowed.

As the days passed in these fruitless activities they had to survive on dwindling stocks of flour and, as recorded by Edgar, a meagre shooting, fishing and trapping bag:

ptarmigan	...	12
weasel	...	4
hare	...	3
fox	...	5

The best of these days was 27 December, and it must have felt almost like a day's sport, with Harold shooting three ptarmigan and Jack two. But it is noteworthy that, for large-scale shooting, they lacked a suitable weapon. With a twelve-bore shotgun, even Edgar, never very successful with his rifle, might have been relied upon to bag a few.

Amidst all this anxiety, difficulty and occasional elation, they had observed Christmas by dining on the head of the caribou killed two and a half months earlier and deliberately saved for this day. The centrepiece of the feast was the tongue, the caribou's celebrated delicacy, and it was eaten with a certain guilty relish.

> Christmas Day and although it seems hardly credible I enjoyed the feast as much as any, although we had nothing in sight for tomorrow's breakfast. When we awoke today we had made up our minds to enjoy ourselves as best as the circumstances would permit. Our frugal meals of rich bannock I enjoyed as much as a turkey . . .

The food was washed down with tea – boiled, black and, unless sugar was added, bitter – from tin cups that were becoming increasingly greasy after two months of 'washing' with sand. By comparison with what he would have expected at home, Edgar's was a squalid, impoverished celebration of the most important holiday in his culture. But, as a holiday from their previous rationing, this was a real party, and even included a kind of inebriation, with the caribou-tongue bannocks producing a rush of well-being in the three hungry men. Next day there must have been a hangover, but Edgar is determined to be cheerful and hopeful:

I hope everyone in England has enjoyed today, and at the same time hope to God we Rustle enough grub for a month from now and not wish we had feasted today.

In this period, their tastebuds delighted at any break in the monotony of the food, however brief. The tang, especially, of overripe meat had a particular appeal. On 4 January:

I found a cache of meat we have quite forgotten having not eaten it before owing to not being good but right now we eat it with Relish.

The day before this, Edgar had made a similar find – fourteen whitefish in the snow 'which we had thrown there for bait if wanted!' The roes of these fish, which were eaten on 7 January, 'smell and taste strongly of some overripe cheese but as Rotten as it may be, is as good as eating cheese'.

Though cheerfulness was the iron rule, an essential part of the code by which all three of them had been brought up, they could not keep it up indefinitely. On 6 January, deeper realities begin to break through into the diary.

Today Weather had turned colder but there was sunshine which is certainly much brighter though does not feel warm and only gives a cheery appearance.

This minor chord was struck again following a spat with Harold.

Harold went for a walk up the creek. I think he said nothing all morning before going and never spoke for some time after coming in, which makes things so unpleasant for us. I did very little all day. Only visited hare trap and cut wood.

Harold Adlard's withdrawn behaviour in the first week of January is one of the few fragmentary glimpses the diary affords of his frame of mind and state of health. His physical condition is difficult to estimate. Malnutrition may already have begun to thread its tentacles through his body, with a general malaise that made him feel, as Edgar had put it on another day, 'not quite the ticket'. But there is an unprecedented note of criticism from Edgar in his diary entry about Harold's silence, as if he could and should have pulled himself together.

A touch of cabin fever, after long hours cooped up indoors, looks likely. Anxiety, depression and brooding cannot be ruled out and Harold may even have begun to find Jack, though superficially so amusing, increasingly difficult to take. Listening to the man's endless boasting, yarning and theorizing, watching Edgar's passionate devotion to his cousin, he must have felt excluded, marooned in the wilderness with a man and a boy who were completely wrapped up in each other.

Cabin fever is a condition eloquently described by the trapper Erik Munsterhjelm:

The continuous presence of another person breeds a loathing for them that eventually develops into hate.

And idleness aggravates the malady tenfold. A gesture or mannerism frequently repeated; the way the other person cuts a slice of bread or rolls a smoke or turns a leaf in a book, his opinions and expressions irritate past all reason . . . Karl had a way of methodically stacking tins on the shelf when he was cooking that made my skin creep. And, if he lay on his bunk, it irked me . . . Both of us enjoyed being as unpleasant and offensive to the other as we dared. The best cure was, of course, to go out and work or hunt but in the bitter cold one did not want to go out for very long.

Critchell-Bullock's diary of his winter with Jack, in their 'house' measuring seven foot by ten, and only six foot six inches high, shows signs of the condition.

11 December 1924. Everything cramped, unget-at-able and wretched. So cold had to put on winter clothing in house. This in case I ever think of it as not foolish and detestably uncomfortable.

16 December. Poor H. is becoming daily more untidy. His only care is in setting traps, cutting up meat and chasing and talking about caribou. Apparently my elaborate equipment is going to be wasted.

19 December. Feeling rather pepperish as H. inclined to be too communistic at times. This rich and poor stuff gets me. He loves talking about this country but should one ever mention any other he will immediately open a book.

8 January. H. has a pocket knife! He uses it for everything, foxes, wolves, bannock, candles, anything. I do
not mind some things. I do object to seeing him cutting
up my meat with it. I objected this evening and the
result is we are not particularly communicative.

In its acute form, cabin fever could lead men into a mutual,
even murderous, paranoia. On their way north in 1911, the
Douglases had stumbled on a remote shack in which lay the
decomposed corpses of two trappers, 'one with his head a
shapeless mass'. Beside this body they found a near-illiterate
note, making it clear its author had shot his companion dead
before blowing his own brains out.

> Cruel treatment drove me to kill Peat. Everything is
> wrong he never paid one sent . . . I have been sick a
> long time I am not crasey but sutnly goded to death he
> thot I had more money than I had and has been trying
> to find it. I tried to get him to go after medison but cod
> not he wanted me to die first so good by. I have just
> killed the man that was killing me so good by and god
> bless you all I am ofle weak bin down since the last of
> March so thare hant no but death for me

The publication of Edgar's diary prompted Critchell-Bullock
to remember his rows with Jack in 1924–5 and, writing to
Colonel Christian, he referred to them in rather tactless terms:

> Hornby and I used to scrap a bit between ourselves;
> but that was when we had the energy to scrap on. When

it became touch and go there was no trouble. If there had been, there would have been a killing.

Harold had now possibly begun to find Jack as hard to take in his daily habits as Critchell-Bullock. The captain's diary graphically describes Jack's way of doing things, as if deliberately to challenge the sensibilities of others.

Hornby regularly eats raw caribou marrow, cracking bones noisily with a large dirty hunting knife sitting amongst the most awful mess of blood, sinew, and untidiness imaginable. Apparently the dirtier the job the more he relishes the product, particularly if his hands are a mess of blood and hawk entrails.

And what was on his hands would also be on his bed, where he often gutted and cleaned carcasses. Keeping clean was never a high priority for Jack in the Barren Ground, because he believed the intense cold nullified dirt. He always maintained that washing was unnecessary there. But his descent into squalor went much further because, caring nothing for comfort, he actively sought its opposite. Critchell-Bullock's diary records:

Of all the uncomfortable trips I have ever had this is the most uncomfortable. Never would I allow H. to arrange for my welfare again.

Jack's insomnia had also infuriated his companion. It was seen as a symptom of his inability to regularize his habits or live according to even the most simple timetable. And in conversation, Jack could be maddeningly oblique and inconsequential, throwing out assertions purely to stir up trouble or to provoke an argument, as once with Critchell-Bullock when:

> H. informed me today that he lives up to the teachings
> of the Christian religion more than any other man he
> has ever met.

If questioned about his way of doing things, Jack might one day refuse to explain himself, and another pile explanations on top of each other in such a way as to smother the question with rationalizations. Any or all of these might be spurious. Harold would no doubt regard it as his right to have straight answers, but straight was not Jack's way. Edgar, in his turn, must have seen Harold as challenging their leader's competence – an unforgivable solecism, in his eyes. His remark 'which makes things so unpleasant for us' has all the wounded priggishness of a schoolboy.

However, even Edgar pressed Jack to tell them when the caribou would return, whether there would be more foxes, in what month the river would thaw. And, the most pressing question of all, how soon would the weather turn? Jack told him not to hope for caribou until the end of March. The foxes would come back with them, but the thaw would not be for another four months. January, which froze the skin, also immobilized the animals. It was the most terrible month in the North and the most critical. After that, conditions would continue to swing considerably between fair and foul, but they could expect a gradual improvement. 15 May, aeons away, was the first day of spring. Then, migrating birds would be seen again.

In keeping with Jack's predictions, the first two weeks following their abandonment of net-fishing were lean. All three were virtually pinned indoors for two days and on the third, 12 January, they took stock anew.

> We all measured out grub today. We have 8 cups [of fat] each per month for 2 months and enough flour for 20 days at the present Rate. Meat for 1 day and bones.

Three days later, the weather was milder (−10°F), but the traps were snowed up and there was still no game to be shot. Jack gave a demonstration of how to extract nutrition from bones. Smashing and pounding with a hammer, he slowly ground them into bonemeal which, when boiled, 'gave off quite a nice cupful of grease' as well as a few mouthfuls of 'gristle'. Unpalatable though this appeared, the bone marrow was full of concentrated nutrients, making an excellent dish in the circumstances.

The temperature continued to fluctuate, plunging one day to −30°F and next day bouncing back to 19°F. 16 January was 'the worst of all days, a strong North wind and −33 all day', but it was not quite, in fact, the worst. The cold gales lasted another three weeks, the nadir coming on 22 January when the thermometer's column shrank below −54°F.

Through all this, there seems to have been no repetition of Harold's sulk. He was busy whenever possible. He checked his traps every two days, and was the most successful of the three at hunting. On 27 January he shot five ptarmigan and, even more significantly, reported seeing wolf tracks crossing the creek.

Jack was galvanized. Wolf meant caribou and tomorrow they might see some. At last the weather, though cold, relented sufficiently to make scouting possible. Then, on 1 February, Harold came in with sensational news.

> A great day of feasting. Harold went out near house and saw Caribou crossing River going North. He eventually shot 1 and wounded 1. Jack and I went out at dusk to bring in meat to make sure it does not get cleared up by wolves. Got back long after Dark with heavy packs. Strong wind at −30 and bad snowdrifts. Having a great feast now and tomorrow we hope to get the wounded animal and calf.

Harold had seen a group of two adults and a calf and stalked them uphill through the woods before making his kill on the Barrens. This confirmation of Jack's prediction that, after January, there would be an improvement was too prompt to be true. But they were not quibbling and Edgar was in a bullish mood:

> Now we have grub on hand things are better and gives one a chance to have a damn good square meal even if we go shy a little later on.

In spite of the fact that both he and Harold had had a touch of frostbite on their noses, there is a triumphant overtone in this restatement of Jack's 'feast-and-famine' mantra. But it was premature. All attempts over the next few days to find the wounded cow and its calf failed. A watch was kept on the river crossing place but there were no more caribou tracks. The meat they had – the caribou and a fat hare trapped in the meantime by Edgar – ran out on 6 February, when 'again we are on the eve of our previous Ration of small flour and sugar'.

Kept going by the recent meat, but burning the energy it gave too fast, they roamed the Barrens and the riverbank yet saw no further caribou. Harold then took to his bunk with a worrying attack of frostbite while the other two went out, wrapped in blankets like a pair of old Indians, to check the traps. The next meat they got was a solitary fox, caught by Jack on 12 February. Four days later 'we have 12 cups of flour and 20 lbs of Sugar and hides for food now', after which two hares and a wolverine just about kept them going for a further week. Edgar allowed himself a rare outburst of frustration: 'This game of going short of grub is hell.' Then, on 22 February, there was more trouble between Jack and Harold.

A nice warm day and Harold thinking it warm declined to cut wood as Jack asked him to but suggested going for a walk in the afternoon. Not quite playing the game considering that we have been out on intense cold days all this month and cut wood on the cold days as well while he makes some excuse of his face freezing. Today I stayed in all the time feeling rotten and Jack is in the same condition but took a look for Ptarmigan, seeing none.

But Harold's dissent was entirely and unexpectedly vindicated next day:

> An Exceptionally mild and nice day but even then both
> Jack and I felt cold fixing traps. I brought home 1 fox
> not fat. Harold took a walk over the Barrens and saw a
> band of 40 caribou but could not get near them at all.

Yet he did so the day after. Charging their veins with precious sugar, the three of them had fanned out across the Barrens:

> Jack and I returned first feeling played out. Harold
> went on out into the barrens and got 1 young bull so
> this makes things much better.

In the morning, while Edgar did 'chaws', Jack and Harold brought down the meat in very heavy packs, Edgar noticing that Jack seemed 'played out by Evening'. They stayed in for the next two days, while a violent storm blew itself out, and the quiet digestion of fresh meat gave them renewed strength and confidence. Perhaps Edgar was beginning to dread the outdoors, for he exclaims several times how wonderful it felt to be forced to rest. Harold, on the other hand, found it hard. He began to argue against Jack's policy of staying close to base and, by the time the weather moderated, he was rebelling again.

> 2nd March. Weather still mild but good and all got out.
> Great dissappointment that we all visited traps and got
> nothing. Harold went out hours after us and shot 2

189

Ptarmigan on barrens having said he would set traps and Jack said don't shoot Ptarmigan in any case.

For some time Harold had been the most successful hunter of the three and he must have used this fact to reinforce his argument for one more hunting trip to the upriver cache. They knew there were caribou about now, and there might be more upstream. There is a feeling that Jack's agreement was weary, but he did agree.

On 5 March, Edgar waved his two companions off with '1 pot of sugar each and whatever other grub they have will be what little flour there is there or what they hunt. I am well fixed here for several days and hope to catch something in traps.' In fact he shot a ptarmigan which made 'Excellent meal for tea.'

Then, at nightfall on 6 March, Jack unexpectedly reappeared, having left Harold hunting from the cache. He said they would be needing an extra gun and told Edgar he was to come back with him upriver. Edgar, who was finding it increasingly hard to 'buck the cold', was reluctant to go but, on 10 March, after securing the cabin, resetting all the traps and assembling heavy packs for the journey, they set out, talking of the kills they hoped Harold had been making in their absence. During the five-hour walk they took a wolverine from a trap – making Jack's load still heavier – and spotted caribou tracks crossing the river ice from the south-west. But, when they staggered into the outlying camp, they found Harold despondent with only 4 ptarmigan to show and not even a sighting of caribou.

They debated the situation. Each of them was almost

exhausted, half-starved and desperately thin, but they had not come this far to fold before the showdown. Edgar had been summoned to join a rigorous, three-day hunt to the west in search of caribou and musk-oxen, leaving next morning and ranging as far as Grassy Island. They decided to go ahead with this plan. It was a brave gamble. Failure would leave them with few chips to play.

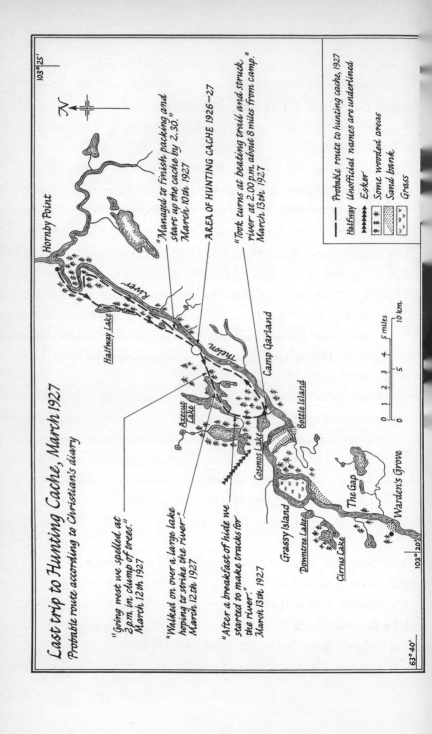

Last trip to Hunting Cache, March 1927
Probable route according to Christian's diary

103° 25′

N

Hornby Point

Halfway Lake

River

"Going west we spelled at 2 p.m. in clump of trees."
March 12th 1927

"Walked on over a large lake hoping to strike the river."
March 12th 1927

"After a breakfast of hide we started to make tracks for the river."
March 13th 1927

"Managed to finish packing and start up the cache by 2.30."
March 10th 1927

AREA OF HUNTING CACHE 1926–27

"Fork turns at beating trail and struck river at 2.00 p.m. about 8 miles from camp."
March 13th 1927

Axecut Lake

Thelon

Camp Garland

Bottle Island

Cosmos Lake

Grassy Island

Downtree Lake

Cirrus Lake

The Gap

Warden's Grove

0 1 2 3 4 5 miles

0   5   10 km.

Probable route to hunting cache, 1927

Halfway Unofficial names are underlined

Esker

Some wooded areas

Sand bank

Grass

103° 20′

63° 40′

14. Death on the Thelon

The planned foray was upriver and would cover the same distance in that direction as they had already travelled from the cabin to the cache. Since it would be necessary to camp out on the trail, the morning of 10 March was spent making up three heavy packs. The start was further delayed by Harold having to mend a snowshoe, which 'he could easily [have] done yesterday'.

Almost immediately after starting out, they were lost. With snow falling and drifting, and visibility a few feet, they were moving blindly.

> Going west we spelled at 2 p.m. in clump of trees and had tea and a little sugar. Here we saw a raven going North so Caribou must be on the move. Before leaving Camp snowstorm got up and we could not see where to travel. During afternoon we walked on over a Large Lake hoping to strike the river.

The big lake was Axecut Lake. If they marched along it, they would cut off a river bend and return to the river, which they could follow up to Grassy Island. Walking over thick lake ice was easier than across the tundra, but nevertheless it took them three hours to reach the lake's end, about four miles away. They were in no condition to travel fast.

> We saw Caribou tracks going North but could get nothing for supper. At 5 pm we pulled in to clump of heavy timber and made Camp then prepared some Caribou hide to eat. I slept a little at night, Jack and Harold were awake all the time.

This wakefulness was deliberate. Snow and wind meant that even in a relatively sheltered grove of trees the temperature at night would fall dangerously low and, if the fire was not kept going, the three men would freeze to death. Jack and Harold had decided to keep each other awake, but it is curious that they did not try a watch system whereby they could have taken turns to sleep singly and guard the fire in pairs. It must have been at Jack's insistence that his cousin, at the others' expense, received a night's sleep.

The Axecut bivouac was at the south-west end of the lake, which was halfway to Grassy Island. But they had already reached the limit of their endurance. Next morning, with the snow still falling, they were

> all feeling tired from want of sleep and little grub, heavy packs and soft snow. After breakfast of hide we started to make tracks for the River. Travelling very bad making packs feel heavier. Took turns beating trail and struck River at 2 pm about 8 miles from Camp. Here we spelled and had a cup of tea and frazzled hide with a little bit of sugar.

They were at the end of their stamina now. The musk-oxen of Grassy Island were forgotten. They realized that a return to the cabin, by way of the cache, had become an urgent priority if they were to preserve their lives.

> We would have a Camp fixed for the night if we got to the Cache and also a hide mat which we could eat and then get back home as soon as possible.

It was a long, painful afternoon's trek, but they made it to the Cache.

> Got in late feeling very tired and I soon fell asleep. Jack and Harold again did not sleep but sat by fire all night.

The next day, 14 March, a 'real Hurricane' blew and they were stormbound. Hunched in their tent, they passed the time 'preparing hide to eat' – the hide 'mat' which had been lodged at the cache in more optimistic days as flooring for the tent. They were just a hair's breadth away from eating boot leather like Franklin. The storm did not abate quickly. After another bad and, for Jack and Harold, almost sleepless night, they finally left on 15 March. They had packed everything they could, including the few remaining reserves of food, into the back-packs or on to the sled. The upriver cache was now officially closed down, with no expectation of its being reopened.

The trek home involved the full sixteen miles by the river bank, since ferocious weather conditions again made the short cut across the Barrens impossible. It was an appalling ordeal. They knew they must make it in a day because another night out could kill them. They travelled on after dark for several hours through soft snow, hauling the laden sled as well as humping big back-packs. Jack fell on the trail and hurt himself 'badly' and, at 8 p.m., the darkness and soft, deep snow forced them to dump all inessential food and kit and carry on with 'bare necessities'. They still did not reach the cabin until 10 o'clock at the earliest – a ten-hour trudge. On arrival, Jack, in spite of his fall,

> was a marvel, Light[ed] fire, made tea and cut firewood.
> I fell asleep about 11.30 and woke at daybreak.

Harold's behaviour on arrival back at the cabin is not recorded.

It was during the following morning that Edgar began for the first time to be seriously concerned about his cousin. While he himself lay recovering in the warm cabin, Jack went out and shot a ptarmigan, but on return he

> looks very poor and must feel it though he will keep
> agoing and doing most work and heavy packs.

Jack's condition was undermined even further by a cruel discovery. He had seen recent traces in the snow of caribou and wolverine passing close to the cabin. It seemed that, while Jack, Harold and Edgar were flailing about on the Barrens, the caribou had come knocking at the door of their empty house.

Each of them must have made his own dire assessment of the previous week. Edgar had taken the pocket diary with him upriver. Now, transcribing the entries into his journal proper, he relived the disaster day by day. The most glaring result had been a further net loss in food stocks. He blamed bad luck and appalling weather, and yet even he must have seen how they themselves had compounded the ill-effects. Jack's double-back to collect him from the cabin was an absurd waste of energy. With only one parka, or capot, between them, their clothing had been inadequate and there was no shotgun for small game. They had lost a quantity of supplies and equipment and the body-mass of each man had been significantly reduced, proportionately sapping his strength. To make matters worse, Jack had injured himself.

How much had their morale been undermined by the failure? Jack's two solitary winters at Reliance had made him acutely aware of the danger that came from disillusion and despair. One night, a few days later, he chose to instruct the others in his experiences there. He dug into his cabin trunk for the typescript of his old Reliance diaries, made for him by Olwen Newell, and read passages aloud to Edgar and Harold, to the accompaniment of a gale howling in the stove-pipe and rattling the door. The pages, and his gaunt bearded face, were lit by a single candle from the cabin's now dwindling stocks. At a time when the mud that caulked the cabin's walls was yet to freeze, Jack had stuck broad English pennies into it and stood a candle on each of them, as the troops used to do in dug-outs on the Somme. Substituting the wailing storm for artillery shells, the present scene might well have conjured memories of night time in the trenches. But even more, it reminded Jack of Fort Hornby, which he had built with his own hands and where he had almost left his bones.

Given the circumstances under which Jack was reading

from them, the Fort Hornby diaries can have been far from entertaining. One passage reads:

> For five weeks I have been listening to the constant begging of the Indians. They say they are starving, and I suppose they are short of victuals owing to the failure of the caribou to pass but certainly they are not on such reduced commons as I am ... I am now practically destitute ... The urge to get furs blinded me to the consequence of running short of supplies so that now I have only 15 lb of flour left ... Tonight I shall have to put everything in order in case anything happens. It is very easy to lie down and give up but an entirely different matter to bestir oneself and move about.

Perhaps the point of the reading was just this: to teach a lesson in determination and point a cheerful moral. Jack, after all, had on that occasion come through, and so would the three of them now. But unless he severely edited his text, it would be very difficult to miss the vital difference. At Reliance, Jack had been saved by the penitent Indians, who came back and gave him food, repaying what they had previously stolen. Here there were no Indians, no trappers, no prospect of relief while winter lasted. The only help possible would come by their own efforts. Otherwise they would starve.

Starvation is a series of vicious cycles. Initially, the body copes well with a reduction in food intake – so well that it might have been designed to do so. 'Inessential' biochemical processes, including inflammatory and immune responses, are curtailed. Subcutaneous fat and muscle mass are burned off to compensate for the inadequate food intake and peristalsis or pulsing of the gut slows down so that what food there is is more efficiently digested. Meanwhile, changes in sodium chemistry within the muscle tissue cause more rapid muscle fatigue, discouraging the voluntary waste of energy. The most visible effect at this stage is the gradual wasting of the body: the hollow-cheeked, big-eyed appearance of the face, the parched or lined skin, the lassitude and the increasingly stiff-jointed gait of the starving man.

But if the food deficit continues, the body begins to lose control. Blood volume and oxygen circulation drop significantly, bringing increased tiredness, both mental and physical. The kidneys start to malfunction so that fluid builds up in the tissue, typically in the lower limbs and, later, on the cheeks, making the sufferer appear – grotesquely – to be getting fat again. Meanwhile, the gut is progressively becoming less efficient. Around its sluggish contents there appears an overgrowth of the gut bacteria whose numbers are normally stable. This not only returns more infections and poisons into the blood, it damages the synthesis of bile salts essential to efficient food absorption. The body is now beginning both to poison itself and to collude in its own starvation. Appetite shrinks. Opportunistic infections, thriving against a background of less resistance, are the more debilitating because their normal external signs and symptoms – swelling, fever – are suppressed. So, on top of his malnutrition, the starving man may, entirely without knowing it, be suffering a variety of common ailments and injuries, which merely weaken him further. Meanwhile, his liver gradually enlarges and his heart, as a result of reduced blood volume, pumps at an increased rate. It becomes a matter of which will strike first, liver failure or congestive heart failure.

It was now April, and with Jack, Edgar and Harold eating almost nothing but small amounts of hide and some bonemeal, these effects were stealing up remorselessly on them. In the beginning, tiredness was the most noticeable problem, since it reduced their capacity for hunting and wood chopping. But the body's declining ability to heal itself was also causing misery. Jack's left leg began to give him increasing pain after 1 April. Probably it was a complication of the injury he had sustained on the way back from the upriver cache, but it may also have been the bone he'd broken way back in 1920, celebrating the Hudson's Bay Company centenary at Fort Smith with a football match. If this break had never properly reunited – which is quite likely in the light of Jack's splinted canoe trip to Fort Reliance – his starvation might by now have caused it to develop the serious and painful condition of osteomyelitis, an abscess in the marrow which, when fully developed, spreads infection to other parts, most typically the throat. Alternatively, this may have been the onset of early gangrene, while a third, even more ominous possibility, is that he had developed scurvy, whose effects include internal bleeding around the bones and into the joints. This too can be severely painful.

They had nothing to eat now but four old wolverine hides, and scraps of refuse such as fish skins and guts which they dug out of the snow. But Jack would not contemplate defeat.

He had become obsessed with the fact that, when Harold had killed his caribou on 1 February, they had jointed the carcass and left the paunch on the barrens. Jack could talk of little else. It would, he said, be frozen deep in the snow, safe enough from predators. If they got it in, they could eat it for days. On 2 April he staggered up to the place and came back with some frozen blood, 'which made an excellent snack', but could not find the paunch. Two days later, he vowed to go out again and continue the search.

Edgar was torn apart. He was certain Jack could not survive this second attempt and tried to dissuade his cousin from it. But Jack was adamant, though he was perfectly aware of the toll it would exact.

Jack kept on Saying he would be all in and absolutely crocked when he Eventually got home again and that we would have to carry on. What a mental strain it was. I felt homesick as never before and hope to God they know not what Jack is suffering. I rubbed his Leg amidst tears and he had saved a little fox meat for me to eat. This cheered me up. I suppose I was crumbling up because of no grub but still by midday Jack started, all muffled up Looking as Cold as Charity and could hardly walk – I wish I could buck the cold more and share his hardships but he has a mind and will of his own and one which no one else has got. I now sit here with Harold frying up bits of fish to Eat and wait for Jack who by now must be icy cold in the barrens.

That he was. He was out in the snow for four hours, heaving himself from drift to drift, taking ten minutes to cross a simple gully or round a fallen tree, clambering tortoise-like up and then down the wooded hillside. Out on the Barrens at last, he crept in circles around the place where he thought the paunch was, poking the snow. But when at last Jack hobbled back into the cabin, he was empty handed. He had not located the caribou paunch. It must have been taken by a wolverine.

In terms of heroism, 4 April must rank high amongst the many great feats of his career. For a dying man to undertake a return six-mile journey on foot, alone and in deep snow, was an act of extraordinary courage and determination. But it was the last of Jack's heroics. Life would continue to flicker for the time being in his body but, as a force, he was now effectively spent. Seeming to know and accept this, he was suddenly infused with a new serenity, the consolation of the dying man. As Edgar wrote:

> Jack feels content to have got back and done as he did and this makes us all feel better and more optimistic as there must be a burst in the weather soon.

In Harold's case, the brighter mood did not last. By now, to accompany his physical decline, he had begun to fall psychologically apart. On 31 March he was 'very grumpy all day and seems to think he is ill so Jack made him get out and get wood and we two had a good rest'. The day after this, Edgar, hardly more sympathetic to Harold in the light of Jack's painful leg, comments that 'Harold getting wood and water says he feels rotten.' He adds caustically, 'So do we!' Over the next few days, Edgar becomes increasingly exasperated with Harold's collapse, which does not seem (as far as Edgar can see) to have any physical cause. On 5 April, the day after Jack's attempt on the caribou paunch, 'Harold talks like an old Woman all day in the house and awful worry to Jack who is the only one Really suffering pain.' Next day, he is no better:

Affairs none too good today. Harold woke up complaining of bad weather to get out and dig in snow for scraps. He said he felt rotten and miserable etc etc. This is an awful selfish way to go on when Jack is suffering and takes long walks when possible. Jack had to curse Harold Eventually to stop his carrying on and it was Like Water on a duck's back.

Edgar here is still blocking out the seriousness of Harold's state, which he sees as not very different from his own. At this stage he himself felt reasonably all right, and he clung to the thought that pluck – if only he had more of it – could see Harold through also.

[Harold] is very queer at times now and one must keep an eye on him at all times till we get grub. Poor devil must be feeling bad but we all are feeling just the same and I find it hell to move around at all . . .

April 7th. Very warm all day but we are so weak and feeble that the slightest wind stops us moving around to hunt. Harold not normal today and thinks he is very bad but if he would only use some willpower to pull through and be more cheery it would make it better for Jack.

The thought that both older men were now becoming 'crocked up' was horrifying and the boy tried to suppress it. He had been in many ways a passenger for much of the last few months, while Harold and (especially) Jack assumed a relatively greater burden of work and the debility that was its consequence. Edgar, wondering if he had continually been let off lightly – and wondering too if Harold's hostility came from this – had already (on 2 April) resolved to be more effective. 'Tomorrow I hope to set 2 hare traps down River and 2 fox traps at same time. See if any Ptarmigan on island.' He seems to have had less physical symptoms than the other two at this stage, beyond tiredness and a peculiar sudden aversion to drinking tea. But his mental distress at Jack's condition had begun to break through. He did not, in fact, set any more traps for another week.

There now began a sharp precipitation towards crisis. On 6 April, Jack 'took a walk and looked for Ptarmigan but got nothing'. It was his last venture out of doors. On 7 and again on 10 April he talked of going out once again after the caribou paunch on the Barrens, but this was pure fantasy. All the while, Edgar devotedly sat by Jack and massaged his painful leg as best he could. With their weakness, and an increased sense of the cold, Edgar and Harold were unable to fell any trees, and had been gradually dismantling the cache next to the cabin, burning its wood in the stove round the clock to keep warm. Cold was not, however, a problem for Jack. He lay in his bunk sweating, having begun to lose control over his body temperature. In medical terms this is *poikilothermia*, in which even slight changes in ambient temperature can trigger either a fever or hypothermia. It is a common symptom of acute starvation.

On 9 April:

Harold is an awful worry saying how bad he is. As far as Looks go the fittest of the bunch of us, but he is too damned afraid of himself and consequently plays another person down.

In the way Edgar expresses this — 'too damned afraid of himself' — one can hear Jack's enfeebled, whispering voice close to Edgar's ear. Jack knew now for certain that he would die, and the next day he asked for paper and a pen. Edgar tore a page from his notebook and Jack wrote carefully in a hand with not a trace of tremor:

The last statement of John Hornby. I hereby bequeath to Edgar Vernon Christian every thing I may die possessed of & all which might later come. April 10 1927. Witnessed by Edgar Vernon Christian and Harold Challoner Adlard.

Over the next few days, he found the strength to write six very short letters. To Colonel Christian:

A farewell line. Edgar is a perfect gem. Our hardships have been terrible & protracted.

To Marguerite Christian:

I am now laid up in bed, writing this note, which may be the last from me . . . Poor Edgar needs a long rest. He has been a perfect companion. He is made of sound material & brought [up] by a perfect Mother. I trust he returns safely.

There were also brief notes to his aunt in Blackburn and to his maiden aunts, Margaret and Annette Hornby, at 34 Ennismore Gardens, Kensington. Each of these is subscribed in Jack's invariable way, 'Yours V. Affect.' There were also letters to his brother and mother which have not survived.

He began to instruct Edgar and Harold in 'what should be done' without him. He told them he might live only two days more. Harold could still walk and was the better shot, so he should go out as much as possible after game – and to bring in that caribou paunch. Meanwhile he told Edgar to reserve his strength for the arrival of caribou from across the river 'in a day or so' and to look out for birds passing over from the south – the first signs of spring. He himself was now as helpless as a baby and utterly dependent on Edgar's nursing. The only food they had were five wolverine hides.

Jack was becoming obsessed with his constipation. It had been a problem for all of them over the last few weeks, and they were convinced that the matter clogging their guts – in particular, the bonemeal they had eaten – was slowly poisoning them. To counter these effects, they had improvised an enema-syringe from a glass test tube and its use became essential to them all. But for Jack, even with this aid, the effort of passing matter from the gut was too exhausting. By the night of 14–15 April, his bound-up state was his only preoccupation and Edgar had the task of administering enema after enema. They seemed to do no good.

Yet, oddly, Jack became 'cheery' and euphoric, and this seemed appropriate when, very early the next morning, Harold shot a ptarmigan, the first fresh meat they had got since 30 March. It was 'simply wonderful of him really but alas Jack is too far gone now to Enjoy such a meal'. By ten-thirty on 16 April, Jack was in and out of consciousness, and at four-thirty he was 'still breathing but unconscious'. The end came at a quarter to seven in the evening, when:

> Poor Jack passed peacefully away. Until that moment I think I remained the same but then I was a wreck. Harold good pal was a Marvel in Helping me and putting things a little straight for the night. I managed to cut some wood by Dark and Harold promised to do the Rest.

Immediately he realized Jack was dead, Edgar crumpled. Harold was deeply touched by the distress he saw and, cancelling out all the hard words spoken in the recent weeks, was compelled to comfort him.

> He talked to me so wonderfully and Realized my Condition I am sure. I Lay on my bed and Listened to him

talk and occasionally I dozed off feeling so worn out. He kept fire during night and brought me tea and Aspirin to help along which was a relief as I was able to sleep.

15. Alone

At one p.m. next day, 17 April, Edgar roused himself to record the details of Jack's last hours. He added:

> Today Harold and [I] are do[ing] just the Essentials and I am looking over certain things as well.

The 'certain things' were perhaps Jack's will, his farewell letters and other papers. Edgar was in deep shock and could do very little of substance, so it was Harold who took care of the most pressing essentials – getting the corpse off the bed and on to a burlap groundsheet, and covering it with a grimy Hudson's Bay Company blanket. The skeletal body cannot have been heavy or taken up much space on the floor. Unable to look at him in death, Harold had already closed Jack's eyes and enveloped his head in one of the expensive Copeland's shirts, monogrammed with not Jack's but his father's initials – 'A. N. H.'. Now Harold parcelled Jack in the groundsheet, which was then meticulously sewed up to make a shroud, though the end of the needle must have hurt his bony fingers. He shuffled the body towards the door and heaved it carefully outside, aligning it closely with the cabin wall, on the side of the door without a window. Edgar does not describe any of this. He does not say if they tried – regretting now the Prayer Book and Bible left in Edmonton

– to recite from memory bits of the Church of England's service of burial. Nor does he record any words spoken over the body. Perhaps he blocked it all out. Perhaps he had been too shocked to say anything. He could not have done better than to use the words of tribute he confided later in the evening to his diary:

> We both are very weak but more cheery and determined to pull through and go out to let the World know of the Last days of the finest Man I have Ever known and one who has made a foundation to build my Life upon.

He was thinking of his father's letters: 'You will have great hardships probably . . . things very seldom turn out as we hope . . . hard work, renunciation & sacrifice & patience.' So now it was a question of simple continuation. As the shock of Jack's death wore off, such a course came automatically to Edgar, who was in character naturally bovine. In the case of the more saturnine Harold, the issue was less simple. For the first twenty-four hours without Jack, and with Edgar incoherent in his grief, he had risen courageously to the challenge of providing support and maintaining hope. But, over the longer haul, he was not up to the effort.

As soon as Edgar was able to appraise Harold with any clarity, he was forced to admit the man looked bad.

> April 18th . . . Harold after doing so well in helping me yesterday fixing up is simply played out . . .

> April 19th. Again the weather is still Cold which keeps

us in all day. Harold is in bed feeling ill and says he has a chill. I do hope he gets well soon . . .

April 20th. From bad to worse Conditions go on. Harold is very weak indeed today and can hardly swallow his food. What is a matter I simply cannot make out for I am able to keep on my Legs and get Wood on the same food of boiled Wolverine hide.

What was the difference? Why was Harold lying prostrate while Edgar could still walk? Harold knew why and, if he made a response to Edgar's pained and frightened questions, one can imagine its acid tone. What was the matter with him? *He* was dying, Edgar was not. On the next page Edgar showed that he, too, had grasped this uncomfortable truth.

Poor Harold is thin and weak and I am not so thin or weak yet have been doing actually more the last few days as regards physical Exertion goes.

Much of the exertion of both men was directed towards excretion. In the diary for this period, entries become longer and more personal as the diarist's capacity for physical work dwindles and his spare time increases. In these entries, Edgar's and Harold's obsession with being 'bound up' is a daily recurring theme. They agree on attributing their chronic constipation to having eaten ground-up bones and wolverine hair, which they believed had combined to block their guts. The discomfort must have been exacerbated by the painful build-up of gas in the intestine, which made their stomachs swell. They formed the conviction that, if only they could properly clear themselves out, they would not only be more comfortable but have more strength for getting food. As it was, they wasted much futile effort on using the home-made syringe, and on straining to produce their paltry stools. This, as Edgar observed of Harold, 'takes every atom of Energy and will power on his part to carry out'.

Otherwise, Edgar felt paradoxically in control of himself at this time. He racked his memory to think of places along the river bank where they had gutted fish in the autumn. He ventured out to dig in the snow, finding skins, skeletons and guts and even odd pieces of meat here and there. Once they suddenly remembered where the remains of one of the pet foxes had been thrown away back in December. Edgar went out and came back triumphantly with the body and it 'certainly was satisfactory and the flesh seemed good'. He also managed to keep the stove going by pulling down more of the log storehouse.

These were flurries of activity, interrupting days that were generally passed in increased lethargy. The two would sit or lie, trying to get their protruding bones in a comfortable position, sleeping and waking in snatches, too tired and dispirited to talk much or do anything. Nutritional anaemia now contributed to the overall debility from wasting, occult infections, kidney failure and the multiple other signs of starvation. They generally had no appetite, except Edgar once, immediately after eating the fox and giving himself a successful enema, when he

Got Rid of a quantity of matted hair off Wolverine hide we must have been eating lately. Not only this fact seemed a change but my appetite was simply Ravenous which it was not so much when eating Hide and this I put down to being bound up of course.

But Harold got out of his bunk less and less and was effectively bedridden by 27 April when, in the morning, Edgar noticed a marked change in him.

Having fixed up Harold's bed he rested better at night but is very weak, especially on Left side. Harold managed to Relieve himself but myself could not.

This left-sided weakness suggests that Harold may now have sustained a mild stroke, brought on by the effects of starvation, which include the release of random blood clots into the arteries. At all events, his condition lurched downwards and the next week was such a strain on both of them that Edgar could not write in his diary at all. Harold, feeling progressively worse, was hardly able to exert himself or eat, while Edgar desperately sought ways to feed his companion by digging for foodscraps, and helped as best he could with enemas. On 2 May, Harold had a 'bad relapse', which was perhaps a second stroke, or possibly heart failure. It was at any rate a mortal blow and, though he rallied somewhat next day, he grew worse in the evening, lapsing in and out of consciousness until 'at 10.5 p.m. Dear Harold passed away'.

*

Edgar's reporting of Harold's death is quite different in kind from the way he had written about Jack's. There is no sense of shock, but instead a show of rational explanation in which Edgar seems almost to enjoy playing the part of a doctor or pathologist. His chief interest, once again, is in bowel movements. Earlier in the day, he writes, Harold

> seemed to get better and wanted to relieve himself. This was managed as usual each day except the previous one and the result was pounded bones again Proving I think that bones have been the trouble all along. After this he was able to move around in bed much more and said he felt better and had shaken off the illness but felt weak so I went out to cut Wood and get water.

Harold's announcement that he had 'shaken off the illness' is puzzling until we remember Jack's euphoria when he, too, had only a few hours to live.

> When I came back he said he felt very queer and knew not what to do although not painful. By 10.5 he had gone unconscious and Slept.

The sleep had no awakening. Now Edgar was alone.

Harold's death certificate states that he died on 4 May, but this is incorrect. The fourth of the month was the day on which Edgar resumed the diary, broken off a week earlier at the start of Harold's final crisis, and it clearly states that death came just after ten the previous evening, 3 May. On realizing that Harold had expired, Edgar seems to have immediately arranged the body on the bunk, closing the eyes, crossing the arms over the chest and covering it. Exhausted, he could do no more. He crawled into his own bunk and slipped into the indescribable relief of sleep. It was only on the next day that he started, slowly and deliberately, to 'fix things as best as possible'.

He cannot have lifted the body, but must have rolled it off the bunk and on to Harold's Hudson's Bay Company blanket, spread out on the floor. He straightened it and wrapped the blanket around. But there was no second canvas groundsheet and Edgar used packing twine to tie the blanket in place. He then dragged Harold's remains to the door and somehow got them outside. He laid them beside Jack, head-to-toe, and said such prayers or words as would come to him. Then he went back in. There were chores to do, wood to get in, food scraps to find and to cook up. Life – in whatever dilapidated condition – had to be resumed.

In the days immediately following Harold's death, though he does not actually say as much, Edgar seems to have renewed his vow of survival. He would tell the world of Jack's heroism and the way in which all three of them had struggled to live on the Thelon in spite of the elemental forces of winter. His own survival would sanctify Jack's death, because it would enable Edgar to bear public witness to his cousin's courage, endurance and self-sacrifice, rather as he had seen Teddy Evans do for Scott at Dover College. In this connection the diary takes on an increased importance for him. It is, of course, his only friend ('Having no one to talk to I must Relieve the desire by writing my thoughts'), but it is also a witness, indeed a monument, to the events he has been living through and to 'the finest Man I have Ever known'.

For several days he fought with much courage to secure his life. He determined to forget about his own tiredness and pain and to focus on objectives – alertness at all times, effort when required, conservation of energy. But he is realistic – 'I cannot hunt as walking around in soft snow is beyond my Powers now' – and he accepts without question – indeed with some enthusiasm – the demeaning activity of digging for refuse which was, given his continuing prejudice against bones and wolverine hide, his last remaining source of food. On 5 May he writes:

> again had luck in finding more good food which had been discarded. 1 very fat wolverine Gut + Kidneys and heart and liver and 1 fox gut. A quantity of meaty bones enough fish for 1 meal. Seeing how bad the Weather apparently is for this time of year I must Safe [*sic*] all the food I can to carry me as long as possible.

And the diary adopts a noticeably brisker tone as Edgar takes stock:

> I now have, Guts 1 day, heart and liver 1 day, meat scrapings 2 days and bone boils to go along with anything insufficiently greasy.

These passages also reveal an additional and increasingly nagging preoccupation with preparedness. He worked to put food aside against contingencies. He constantly kept an eye out for the migrating birds that would signal the longed-for spring. And, though he had accepted his reduction, for the time being, to the status of scavenger and carrion-eater, no higher in the food chain than the despised wolverine and whisky-jack, he still had the means and the foresight to be a hunter should the chance arise. Moving as slowly as he now did, it would be unfortunate if he should hear an animal outside and be unable to bring his weapon to bear quickly enough. So he loaded all three rifles and propped two of them against the cabin wall just outside the door. He kept the third inside, for pot shots through the window.

The 'improved' food he obtained from digging with the small hand axe in the snow – he had now found a rich refuse pile which had accumulated during the relatively plentiful days of early winter – had a paradoxical effect. With a stock of offal that he could eat 'with Relish', and which certainly had more nutritional variety than he had recently been used to, he went to bed on 6 May and slept for more than ten hours. When he woke, his mind was clear, and in some way perceptually refreshed, so that it was all the more disturbing that it should deliver such a nasty shock to him.

> I felt much fitter but to my Surprise I was as thin as a Rake about my Rump and my joints seemed to jerk in and out of position instead of smoothly.

He is describing in almost classical terms the condition of the limbs and joints of a starving man. Ligaments lose their tone, the joints are loosened and become unstable, muscle bulk and body fat waste away, the knee, hip and arm joints lose all cushioning. This gives the alarming jerkiness, the sense of bone grinding on bone, which suddenly and for the first time came to Edgar's attention when he tried to stand or walk. None of this had happened to him overnight. It had been a minute erosion over a period of many weeks, though only now did he become aware of it. Starvation, so stealthy and accompanied by so many emotional and perceptual distortions, often misleads sufferers into denying the evidence of their senses. The human skeleton is not meant to be seen or felt. To be forced suddenly into an awareness of one's bones jarring against each other or pushing out against the suddenly baggy skin is too frightening. In its way, Edgar's explanation of the phenomenon – which is obviously attributable to nothing but starvation – is a curious continuation of this denial.

> This [instability in the joints] I believe to be exactly the same thing as happened to poor Jack and Harold through walking on Snowshoes when their systems were full of pounded bones.

His fixation on what he could evacuate from his body, as great as his interest in what he fed into it, continued. Almost daily he used the enema syringe loaded with 'soap and hot water' and, though the results were variable, the intention was always the same – 'to clear my System' of bones. Having written on this subject at some length on the morning of 7 May, it occurred to him that some readers – if there ever were to be any – might think he had become obsessed.

I write all this down as I think it is of importance see-ing how Suddenly Harold and Jack went ill, but I must stick to my guns and Endeavour to cure myself now.

Sticking to his guns, the metaphor bringing with it a new recollection of his father, was mandatory now. It was not bravery but duty. *Non recuso laborem.*

But the problem was that his (temporarily) more active mind found no matching revival in his body. Edgar was moving in slow motion all the time and everything he did took five times longer than normal. On 7 May he spent two hours writing a little over 300 journal words. Preparing and administering the enemas also took hours, while his snow-digging for a few morsels of food was interminable. His readiness with the rifles was of limited use when he could not make his body work fast, a fact which came home to him that same day, in late afternoon, when he was

just looking out for the last time and saw 4 ptarmigan feeding in front of the house, had to hurriedly go out and took little Rifle being the lightest. Birds were wild, I could not get close. 1 shot and they went, however hope more come around for they are the first things I have seen for a long time now.

In Edgar's condition this would have been a difficult shot from anything further than point-blank range. The kick of the rifle butt against his bony shoulder must alone have been painful, and once again the thought recurs: the spread-barrel of a shotgun, even if fired from the hip, would have brought him more success.

He blamed snow-digging in wet clothes for the 'chill' which afflicted him next day. As with Jack a month earlier, he developed a fever and lay in his bunk burning and sweating. But he could still get out, and was rewarded with a whisky-jack in one of his traps, 'so had a cup of tea and ate it straight off'. That evening a raven passed over the cabin flying north and Edgar realized there had been more ptarmigan out front, 'while I was pounding bones this morning'.

On 9 May he observed morbid symptoms piling up on him like a heavy portage pack. His chill was no better. Walking was further restricted by a badly hurting back, which he does not try to explain, though it was perhaps a kidney or urinary-tract infection, or even an exacerbation of his earlier injury on 4 December, received whilst carrying logs. He felt unusually cold even though the weather was a mild 10° F. He reports 'success at relieving myself', but 'moving around seems to be a wobbly process'.

On 10 May:

I feel fine keeping warm in the house which needs lots of wood but having to go out and sit chopping for grub just makes my head all hazy and my ears thick and feet cold. I am changing clothes and drying out night and morning and sweating hard at night. Only got enough food for 1 meal today but have enough till the 12th at any Rate. I wish I could only lay to and sweat off my cold and I would be alright I think because with the aid of the Syringe I am clearing my system of foul matter every day, a very weakening process but apparently the only one on such food. I feel very worried and Lonely hoping for fine weather and tonight as it looks like a snowstorm coming I have plenty of wood on hand. My shoulder blades and joints still seem to jerk in and out of place and my nose gives way to bleeding. Appetite not as keen as should [be] on amount I eat. Had a little snack and Cup of tea at midday which leaves me with no more gut fat for little tit bits to fry in, however all good things come to an end someday and I hope I get a jolly good feed of meat one day soon which should put things OK.

'Chopping for grub' was an activity he had now come to dread. But the snow was still, in most places, as deep as ever, although it had retreated here and there where the sun shone. This yielded curious results. Returning laboriously with a few logs on 11 May, Edgar

noticed quite a nice piece of fish lodged in a tree from where the snow had thawed. If only the Weather would get really warm there are lots of bits of this kind [that] would come to light but to dig in several feet of snow in hopes and not a certainty is a waste of Energy just now.

For ten days after Harold's death, Edgar continued faithfully to record temperatures, and although it still froze day and night, there were no more sub-zero readings. Yet Edgar, while noting the daily low and high marks, could not feel it getting warmer. His perception of temperature was a function of his severe malnutrition and bore little relation to the thermometer. 11 May ('10 deg & 10 deg') was a 'very cold day' on which 'as soon as I get outside my ears begin to feel queer which must be cold'. On 12 May ('10 deg & 15 deg') 'weather still cold', and on the next day ('10 deg & 15 deg') he had to 'wrap up' inside and 'the house needs so much wood to keep warm'. After this day, Edgar recorded no more daily readings.

The cessation of weather data in the diary is significant. This had been one of his prime tasks, a gesture towards the expedition's 'scientific' pretensions. Its abandonment signals a real lowering of Edgar's will at this point. However, on 12 May, he was briefly 'feeling much more fit to day, do not seem to have such a cold about my head and appetite very keen. Very unfortunate to feel so hungry but must mean for the good.' This last remark would be quite true if it did not contradict all the other evidence. In starvation, appetite normally diminishes gradually and, by the final stages, evaporates altogether. Edgar's short-lived appetite must have been a mirage, or a demon come back to torment him at a time when it should have been the least of his problems.

By 13 May, Edgar was moving more than ever like a zombie, and now, inexorably, his brain slowed also, as it fumbled with the simplest but starkest dichotomy he had yet faced: that between food and warmth: 'I think it best not to dig today but try and get Strength for wood cutting in the evening.'

Meanwhile, he was sleeping much, picking through the autumn's well-used refuse pile and burning wood chips from around the stumps of trees which they had felled months earlier. He also started feeding the furniture and floorboards into the stove, which thus slowly began to devour Jack's cabin, as it had already consumed the storehouse.

Each day he felt weaker, which puzzled him. He had plenty of food and, though it was all scraps, it was healthier than wolverine hide. On 14 May he remembered what Jack had told him in the depth of winter. The next day was the beginning of spring in the North. He must keep alert.

15 May, with its full moon, passes. The clouds are leaden and the wind blows, more like a reversion to darkest winter than the onset of springtime. Edgar struggles to cut wood for his cooking and tells himself he can and must keep going. But another voice tells him he 'cannot last for ever like this without fresh food'. 16 May is 'just as yesterday only worse. Could not cut wood.' He is reduced to dragging brushwood up from beneath a tree a few yards away and this suffices to:

> cook some fish Scraps for Supper along with hare guts. Tomorrow I will have meat Scrapings for breakfast, probably Wolverine stomach for Supper and hope for the best and burn what I can of furniture.

On 17 May he is again oppressed by the weather and cannot move all day, just sleeps and stares into space. 'If I cannot get grub tomorrow must make preparations.'

But next day, he wakes to a glint of yellow light. Gingerly he rolls from his bunk and on all fours crawls towards the door. The sun is out in a clear blue sky. He shuffles round and surveys the cabin. In a blackened cooking pot he still has bones from the refuse pile, thin dry bones of hares, ptarmigan, fox. He spills them out on to the flat stone he uses for pounding and grips the hammer, his hands like chicken claws. He hammers wearily, each blow calling up reserves of strength he does not know he has. After an interminable time the bones lie before him broken into fragments, though they are far from the bonemeal that Jack achieved after his first demonstration of bone-pounding four months ago. There is water in the pot on the stove and embers inside, so now all he has to do is feed in some wood chips and coax a flame.

These simple activities take up much of the morning. When the bones are boiling Edgar crawls back to the door. He can probably stand but is far more comfortable and secure on all fours. Creakingly, holding the door frame with one hand, he eases himself outside and looks towards the refuse pile which is about twenty yards away, a dirty mound of snow and slush with the hatchet stuck in at the top. He pulls on his mittens and begins to crawl out, pushing a tin bowl in front of him. Suddenly he is aware of movement in the spruce some distance beyond the refuse pile. He sees a ptarmigan fussing around a bare patch of ground from where he had previously recovered certain scraps. He turns and laboriously ploughs back to the cabin. At last he reaches the rifle, propped against the log wall. He grasps the stock of the rifle and, using it as a support, pushes himself into a standing position. But by the time he has turned about, and wrapped his forefinger around the trigger, the bird has disappeared. He carefully reprops the gun, lowers himself cautiously back on to his knees and begins once again the long journey to the refuse pile.

When he gets to the place he pokes at the snow with the axe, though it is heavy and difficult to manipulate. He uncovers a fish skeleton, drops it into the bowl and heaves the hand axe again. He doesn't know what makes him look up. He doesn't think there was a cry or a crump of wings, but something must have prompted him to ignore the pain in his back, though it sears like a hot wire, and twist his body, turning his face upward. Hundreds of feet above him in the pure blue air, a white swan is making its way north. It is almost overhead, the neck like an elegant finger pointing its direction, the wings paddling the air effortlessly. He knows it is a whistling swan on its way to its breeding grounds. He smiles. Jack was right. It is spring.

After one more short entry on the next day, mentioning sun followed by snow, the diary again ceases. For the rest of May we know nothing of Edgar, as his vitality fitfully dims and flickers like one of the few remaining candles guttering on its wall-mounted penny. Then, on 1 June, he stirs himself again. He opens the book, grasps his pen and with infinite care starts to write.

May 20–June 1st. have existed by Walking and Crawling in and out of house finding plenty of food in fact more than I could eat but owing to it[s] quality did not keep me going sufficiently to get Rid of it as I ate it being insufficient in grease I think. On 22nd I found lots of meat under snow and 4 good big meaty bones covered in fat and Grease. These put me on my Legs for 3 days cutting wood etc. and I cooked up enough fish for 4 days and then Rested Thinking I could Lay to and strengthen when the weather might be warmer and I would find more grub thawing out and even shoot ptarmigan if I could walk. Alas got weaker and weather was blowing Snowstorm for 4 days after that and not Even thawing in daytime. Now June 1st. I have grub on hand but weaker than have ever been in my Life and no migration north of bird and animals since 19th (Swan).

Yesterday I was out crawling having cut last piece of wood in house to cook me food I had which is a very fat piece of Caribou hide but while out I found fish and meat in plenty and greasy gut fat on in sides of foxes and Wolverine, containing liver and hearts and Kidneys and Lights 1 fox Carcass. All this I cooked up Leaving the hide as a Cache. I ate all I could and got Rid of much foul food from my system, apparently been stopping me walking. At 2 a.m. went to bed feeling Content and bowl full of fish by me to Eat in Morning.

9 a.m. Weaker than Ever. have Eaten all I can have food on hand but heart peatering. Sunshine is bright now. see if that does any good to me if I get out and bring in wood to make fire to night. Make *preparations* now.

There are just two more lines of writing in the diary and then Edgar brings it to an end:

Got out too weak and all in now. Left Things Late.

When he completed these painstaking lines he had a little additional writing to do. The diary was his public record but he had more personal feelings to communicate also, before it really was too late. He found a sheet of the notepaper from the Windsor Hotel, which he'd purloined on 1 May more than a year ago, scrawled a line through the printed name of the hotel and opened a letter to his father in almost jocular style.

Dear Father: My address is not the above but I hope this finds you one day . . .

He filled the first side of the sheet and turned over. His handwriting was becoming larger and the line more erratic. He finished the letter to his father halfway down the page and began a second to his mother, which ran to only twelve lines. Then he folded the paper and slid it into a hotel envelope. On this he wrote his mother's name and 'The Officers' Mess, Royal Artillery, Portsmouth' before tucking it into the back of the diary.

Slipping amidst jarring pain to the floor, Edgar crawled to the McClary stove, which he had not lit since yesterday. The ashes were cool now and he shoved the book in amongst them. Carefully he gathered more papers together – Jack's will and farewell letters, Harold's 12 August letter to his parents from Sifton Lake, his own pocket diary and a similar one belonging to Harold – all of which he deposited in the firebox. He shut and latched the stove door.

Laboriously, Edgar returned to his suitcase and fumbled for another blank sheet of paper and took up his pen. Laying this on top of the stove, he bent over to write in shaky capital letters:

WHOEVER FINDS THIS LOOK IN STOVE.

Edgar had done with preparations. He crossed to the cabin door and latched it from the inside. He shuffled back, drained by all his efforts, to his bunk. He lay gingerly down and wrapped himself in his red blanket, pulling it high to cover his face. Nothing mattered at all to him now, nor ever would again. He was exhausted. Gratefully, he closed his eyes. He slept.

16. Cold Burial

The Arctic summer came, and went, and bitter cold again encroached on the lifeless cabin. Driven by ferocious autumn storms, snow accumulated in drifts, bending the roof poles, closing up the window holes, clogging the doorstep. The ice arrested everything that moved.

A few curious animals and birds picked their way around the accidental mausoleum, pausing to nose the snow crust, sniffing the few places where organic remains lay frozen deep beneath – fish skins, pelts, human remains, all alike encased in impenetrable ice. There were days when malicious weather raged over the Barren Ground, like the Indians' vengeful Weetigo, its breath cold enough to kill, its bite sharp enough to take a man's nose and fingers. Whenever the storms withdrew, the cabin stood in the sparkling winter sun, cryogenically preserved for another season. Occasionally, a roof-spar cracked, a brief rain of shingle rattled down and new chinks of cold light sprang across the ruined room. One illuminated the cast-iron stove, on top of which lay the decayed sheet of paper with Edgar's final message. Attacked for months by moisture and frost, it had fallen apart and was now incomplete: WHO ... LOOK IN STOVE.

On 21 July 1928, a group of prospectors appeared on the Thelon, travelling downstream in two canvas-covered canoes. The four-man party was led by Harry S. Wilson, a twenty-eight-year-old mining engineer of the Nipissing Mining Company from Cobalt, Ontario. Wilson and his team – John Muirhead, Kenneth Dewar and John Thomson – were intending to make a rapid mineralogical survey of the lower reaches of the Thelon, where it approaches the west side of Hudson Bay.

They knew they were some hundred miles north of the great forests, so it was a surprising pleasure, here on the Thelon, to be gliding at three or four miles an hour past thick groves of willow and spruce growing up the steeply sloping shore. The previous day, ten days after entering the Barrens, they had seen musk-oxen. But apart from a few bankside cairns, there was no evidence of man. Now Thomson, in the leading canoe, pointed to a spot up among the trees on the north shore, where there stood a simple log house of typical trapper's design. Although unmarked on any of the old explorers' maps, it was not entirely unexpected.

On his way north, Wilson had informed the Royal Canadian Mounted Police at Fort Smith of his route and was asked to look out for John Hornby. Now, as he ran his canoes ashore, his first thought was that this must be Hornby's camp. But, as they approached, they realized that the cabin was dilapidated and forsaken. The roof sagged and the window glass was shattered. The door was firmly shut.

They examined the remains of the log store and the two bulging pack sacks filled with animal furs, mostly white fox, which lay nearby. The pelts were badly damaged by grubs. A few rusty or weathered items of camping and trapping equipment were lying around and propped against the cabin wall on each side of the door were the two loaded .303 rifles which Edgar had left in readiness. They were now so rusty as to be useless. Next, against the log wall to one side of the door, they noticed the two tied-up elongated bundles, one of rotten canvas and the other of wool. The latter, though dirty and stained, was identifiably a Hudson's Bay Company blanket.

Dewar opened his clasp knife and probed the decayed material in the nearest bundle until the point was stopped short. He enlarged the hole and carefully separated its edges with his fingers to reveal the brow and eye-socket of Harold Adlard's skull. Grimacing, Dewar looked up at each of his companions. No one spoke. He turned back and made a rent in the other canvas-covered parcel, revealing a portion of Jack's skeleton.

Muirhead tried the cabin door: it was fastened from the inside. He hammered on it, shouting 'Hello! Anyone at home?' The commonplace words echoed startlingly amongst the surrounding trees. Muirhead looked at Wilson, who nodded. Then Muirhead and Thomson put their shoulders to the door and, after several hard shoves, the internal latch broke. The door swung open.

Cautiously they filed in. The air was damp and suffused with a bitter, foul smell. They could see in the middle of the room a cooking pot, partially filled with water, standing on a small box-stove. The skull of an animal, possibly a fox, lay in the water. A roughly made table nailed to the rear wall contained a half-empty packet of tea, some crockery, assorted items of ammunition, two caribou skulls complete with antlers, other bones, medicine bottles, binoculars, camera, film and other detritus. Underfoot were the remains of the floor, most of the boards having been torn up. They saw three mouldering leather suitcases with labels of the Canadian Pacific Railway, a tin trunk and a rattan cabin trunk. There were also the splintered remains of two home-made bunk beds. A third bed stood intact in the north-east corner.

Wilson rummaged in the trunk, lifting out a bundle of the papers and carrying them to the light of the window. Dewar approached the bunk, which was covered with another mouldy Hudson's Bay Company blanket. He grasped the blanket to see what it concealed, but no sooner had he twitched it than he regretted the suddenness of his action. First, with a dry, unnerving rattle, the bare bones of a human foot fell on to the floor. At the other end of the bed, the blanket slid a little way down and a skull toppled sideways, lying for a moment exposed and grinning at Dewar. He swore out loud and they all looked. Briefly they saw tufts of silvery blond hair still adhering to the cranium. Then the entire skeleton toppled sideways, sliding from beneath the decayed blanket and, with a hollow clatter, dropping to the floor.

The four men exchanged glances. Then Wilson stuffed the papers hurriedly back into the trunk and they all scrambled for the door. Within minutes they had regained their canoes and pushed off from the bank.

Further downstream, a little ashamed of their panic, Wilson described the bundle of papers. There were letters and suchlike and he'd spotted the name Hornby several times. It was clear that these really were the three adventurers they'd heard about at Fort Smith. Someone said that the corpse in the cabin had white hair, so it must have been that of the older man, Hornby: he must have died last. There was no thought of going back. Instead, suddenly reminded of their own dwindling supplies and the distance they had to go, they paddled quickly on downstream.

Wilson and his men would not have made the mistake about the body in the cabin if they had read the message tucked under the rusty cooking pot. But the paper had become covered in dirt and was half eaten away by damp and mould. So the visitors never opened the stove door to find, beneath the clammy ash, a notebook whose leather cover still bore the word RECORDS stamped in gold leaf.

Marguerite Christian had realized there could be no news of Edgar and Jack before July 1927, when the winter's ice broke up. But when, even then, no news came, the pleasurable anticipation of seeing her son gradually darkened to anxiety and outright dread. Enquiries that summer in Canada, through Godson-Godson, the Armitsteads, Jack's solicitor Colonel Yardley Weaver, and even the police, yielded little information.

There is no record of any contact with the Adlards, but Harold's family must have written or telephoned, mentioning Harold's letter, in which he stated the intention of staying two years in the Barrens. This information would have provided a lifeline for Marguerite to cling to throughout that second winter. But the year 1928 brought no immediate relief. Colonel Christian had received a new overseas posting, to Hong Kong, but it was decided that Marguerite would stay on at Bron Dirion, with the aim of joining her husband at

Christmas. Edgar would by then be with them too, please God, and they would all be together.

The illusion was shattered on 14 August, when a reporter from the *Daily Mail* came knocking on the door of Bron Dirion. He held in his hand a wired story from Reuters, Ottawa. The journalist may have been embarrassed when he realized that he was the first to break the news to Mrs Christian. But he knew his job. He handed her the paper and watched as she absorbed the information that her son was dead.

George Douglas had always feared the outcome. Unlike Edgar's family, unlike many of the 'old pals' in Edmonton, unlike the *Edmonton Journal*, he knew the terrors of a winter in the Barren Ground and how Jack's eccentricities would be sure to magnify them. But, with his fondness for the man, Douglas also considered his friend an oddly lucky fellow who had faced many mortal dangers in the past – in the Barrens, in France – and had always overcome them.

In the winter of 1926–7, Douglas had written from Clark-dale, Arizona, where he was then working, to Inspector Charles La Nauze of the RCMP at Halifax, Nova Scotia, asking to be informed if and when Jack reappeared. La Nauze wrote back saying that Jack, with his 'two nephews', was 'somewhere around the east end of Great Slave Lake, probably between Resolution and Reliance'. This inaccurate information from 'last fall' must have been given by the trappers Jack had met on the way to Fort Reliance in June 1926. 'The only remark I can add,' wrote La Nauze, 'is Lord help the two nephews.' Yet Douglas must have been encouraged by the possibility that Jack was close to the shores of Great Slave Lake and, like everyone else, he expected to hear further news in mid-1927. When he didn't, he realized that Jack had, after all, ventured into the Barrens proper.

With autumn came persistent rumours of disaster, none substantiated. Then the Ottawa correspondent of the *New York Times* filed a story about Jack, reporting the scuttlebutts going around and the concern of the Department of the Interior. Guy Blanchet, Vilhjalmur Stefansson and James Critchell-Bullock all responded to the story in similar ways, asking who was being sent in search of Jack and his companions. Frustrated at his own impotence during the winter of 1927–8, Douglas sat down to write a personal letter to Jack, with copies going care of police posts at Fort Resolution and Fort Smith:

Dear Hornby: Nothing has been heard of you for so long we are feeling much anxiety about you . . .

I am planning a trip into Great Slave Lake this summer, and should certainly like you to join the party . . . I am keeping a 'space' for you anyway. If this comes to you please let me know by telegram from Smith . . .

Meanwhile, there were tales of three skeletons seen in a boat adrift around Baker Lake and of Indians reporting white men drowned on Artillery Lake. Then there were sightings of Jack, alive and well, as far apart as Medicine Hat in Alberta and Victoria Island in the Arctic. In Edmonton, trappers such as Cooley and the Stewarts were interviewed, both by police and journalists, and with every newspaper article came fresh hyperbole to boost the legend of Hornby: 'Jack Hornby could go further on a diet of snow, air and scenery than a Lizzie can go on twenty gallons of gas' was Cooley's boast to the *Edmonton Journal*.

Fending off a letter from James Critchell-Bullock, in which the captain offered to lead a rescue bid, Administrator Finnie had already made up his mind about the case. After reviewing the latest police reports from Corporal Williams, recently established at the new RCMP post at Fort Reliance, he wrote to Police Commissioner Starnes on 9 August 1928: 'It is beginning to look as if Hornby and his companions have perished somewhere in the vicinity of the Thelon Game Sanctuary.' Finnie did not yet know that H. S. Wilson's party had already made their gruesome discovery. But on the very day that he wrote to Starnes, Wilson was writing out his statement for Staff Sergeant Joyce at Chesterfield Inlet.

On 10 August Joyce wired Ottowa with the news:

> H. S. Wilson here from Great Slave Lake. He reports finding bodies of Hornby party of three men at cabin on North bank of Thelon River about sixty miles below junction of Hanbury and Thelon. Deaths apparently due to starvation. Bodies left as found. Full report on the *Nascopie*, which leaves here 11th.

The *Nascopie* was a vessel plying between Chesterfield Inlet and Montreal, but its progress was slow. By the time Starnes received a hard copy of the report, it was September and the news of Hornby's death was out. By 14 August the *Edmonton Journal* had run the story on its front page:

BODIES OF JACK HORNBY AND TWO
COMPANIONS FOUND IN LONE CABIN

The same day, Reuters had flashed the news to every corner of the world.

Starnes had hoped to send Joyce, an authorized coroner, west from Chesterfield Inlet to investigate the cabin, bury the bodies and recover the dead men's possessions. There was a plane Joyce could borrow but this was under repair and it was already late in the season. The plan was abandoned and it was now decided that nothing could be done before the following spring, when a three-man foot patrol would go into the Thelon from Fort Reliance.

The party, led by Inspector Trundle, left Reliance as soon as the thaw made it possible, arriving at the cabin after a three-week dash on 24 July – more than two years after Edgar's death. Trundle's report, which was eventually reprinted in both published versions of Edgar's diary, is a model of thoroughness. He noted the disposition of the cabin, its contents and the immediate surrounding area. From the interior he collected any possessions that were not worthless, drying out the papers as best he could. He provisionally appropriated the stove to be used at the new game-warden's cabin upstream from Grassy Island, and destroyed everything else, including the rusty rifles. Most important of all, Trundle recovered the diary from the stove and read through it. He does not record any emotion at being Edgar's first reader, commenting only:

> After making this investigation and reading the diary of E. V. Christian, and a cursory examination of the numerous papers, it was decided that an inquest was unnecessary.

Trundle and his men buried the three bodies side by side in front of the cabin, marking the graves with wooden crosses fashioned from the slats of wood Jack had brought in as building material. At the intersection of each cross they etched the initials of the victim, identified with reference to Edgar's diary. After driving in the crosses they stood in a semi-circle with heads bowed while the Inspector read the briefest of burial services. Then they left.

Among the papers perused by Trundle were Edgar's final words on the expedition, the last letters to his parents. After fulfilling his duty by reading them, the policeman had carefully closed them up again, feeling no doubt an acute sense of intrusion into private family grief.

Dear Father

My address is not The above
but I hope this finds you one day.

Jack Hornby always
wished to see this Country sometime
before he gave up The life in aoctic
Regions & wanted someone with him
& I was the one this time. I realise
why he wanted a boy of my age with
him & I realize why one other should
come in order to make sure I got out
safe, but alas the Thelon is not what
it is cracked up to be I dont think. I have
now been trying to struggle by
myself for over a month & help
my other poor pal but Spring is
late here & I cannot get fresh meat
although have always had food to eat
at times some jolly good meals only
a few days ago which did not put me
in condition to hunt fresh food but the
weather blew cold & to day June 1 It
has seen me with fine weather
food but not fresh & unable to get
fresh being too weak & played out

adr
Adamson Carona Hotel Edmonton
finds 2 trunks of mine
& in on that "Bible & Prayer Book
which Jack refused to let me bring
do not be annoyed but I know
why now & Jack alone was one man
in this world who can let a young boy
know what this world & the next and
I loved him he loved me. very seld
is there true love between 2 men!

Bye Bye now Love
& Thanks for all
you have Ever done for
me Edgar.

Dear Mother
feeling weak now can only
write little sorry left it so late but
alas I have struggled hard.
Please don't Blame Dear
Jack the Loves you & me only
In this world & tell no one else
this but keep it & believe.

Ever Loving & Thankful to
you for all a Dear mother
is to a Boy & has been to me
Bye Bye Love to all
& Dulc Rits Fred Charles
& Gwen
Edgar

17. Verdicts

It is evident from Colonel Christian's two farewell letters of April 1926 that he believed there were deeper purposes at work in human destiny. Private grief, painful though it was, remained less important than the hope that Edgar had comported himself at all times courageously and like a gentleman. It was not until they received the diary, with the re-sealed letters Edgar had addressed personally to them, that his parents' hopes in this direction were confirmed.

The letters were particularly precious. The diary was a more public document, and had already been read by others whose job it was to establish the cause of death of the three men. By contrast, the Windsor Hotel envelope contained a direct communication from their son, whose tongue had moistened the gummed flap in the desolate cabin on the Thelon, as the bodies of his friends lay stretched out on the ground outside the door.

His opening words, 'My address is not the above', are the first note of irony struck in any of his writings, and he made no effort to sustain it. Edgar's real concern was to tell his parents that he was resigned to, and did not regret, his fate.

Jack Hornby always wished to see this country sometime before he gave up the Life in Arctic Regions & wanted someone with him & I was the one this time.

241

He seems to imply a sense either of malign destiny or pure accident — 'I was the one this time' — but Edgar quickly moves away from this to end with another, much more meaningful type of justification — an extraordinary declaration of perfect and unqualified love for his cousin.

> I realize why he wanted a boy of my age with him & I realize why one other should come in order to make sure I got out safe, but alas the Thelon is not what it is cracked up to be I dont think. I have now been trying to struggle by myself for over a month & help my other poor pal but Spring is Late here & I cannot get fresh meat although have always had food to eat at times some jolly good meals only a few days ago which did not put me in condition to hunt fresh food but the weather blew cold & today June 1st has seen me with fine weather food but not fresh and unable to get fresh being too weak & played out. Adamson Corona Hotel Edmonton finds 2 trunks of mine & In on[e] that Bible & Prayer Book which Jack refused to let me bring do not be annoyed but I know why now & Jack alone was one man in this world who can Let a young boy know what this world & the next are. I Loved him he Loved me. Very seldom is there true Love between 2 men!
>
> Bye Bye now Love & Thanks for all you have ever done for me
>
> Edgar.

The letter to his mother, shorter and more desperate, is a compressed repetition of the same message, vividly conveying the sense that life was now quickly leaking away.

> Dear Mother: Feeling weak now can only write Little Sorry Left it so Late but alas I have struggled hard.
>
> Please dont Blame Dear Jack. He loves You & me only in this world & tell no one else this but keep it & believe.
>
> Ever Loving & Thankful to you for all a Dear Mother is to a Boy & has been to me. Bye Bye Love to all & Dulc Rits Fred Charles & Gwen
>
> x Edgar

So the expedition, in this stark final moment, did not seem to Edgar to have really failed at all. What had failed was unimportant – the mortal body. In terms of the spirit, and as a testament to comradeship, mutual help and struggle – to human love itself – Edgar could see only what was positive and honourable.

Even in his terminal state, he was clear-sighted enough to see that accusing fingers would be pointed at his cousin: 'Please don't Blame Dear Jack.' For Edgar, blame for what had happened did not enter into the matter. Jack Hornby had been his paradigm of a complete gentleman as well as his mentor, willing to teach the boy everything and to provide a platform on which to build his manhood. Now that furs and rocks and wildlife photographs were quite forgotten, this was revealed as the whole object of the trip. It was their Everest and their Pole. And, even in failure, it honoured their family and their nation, turning physical defeat into moral victory and justifying everything.

Many of those who read the press reports of Edgar's death in 1928 were moved to write letters of condolence to his parents. The majority found an appropriately heroic register for the expression of their sympathy.

> It is boys and men like him that have made England what she is.

> A grand example to the rising generation that the spirit of adventure is not yet departed from the Race.

> He died as a pioneer in a new country and thousands of great Britishers like him have met the same glorious death.

And one correspondent made a parallel with Captain Scott.

> You will always be proud of his achievements and, as Dr [*sic*] Scott the great explorer of the unknown said, English men can endure hardships, help one another and meet death with as great a fortitude as ever in the past.

This correspondent's quotation from Scott of the Antarctic is apposite. It comes from the letters of farewell Scott wrote on the Great Ice Barrier, while he waited in his tent to die.

In these, Scott had mounted a final defence of his actions in defiant words:

> The causes of the disaster are not due to faulty organization but to misfortune in all risks which had to be undertaken . . . I do not regret this journey, which has shown that Englishmen can endure hardships, help one another and meet death with as great a fortitude as ever in the past.

Without the bombast, Edgar's own last sentiments, expressed in the letters to his parents, had been remarkably close to Scott's, with their emphasis on honour, comradeship and courage.

The initial newspaper coverage enthusiastically endorsed these thoughts. While concentrating almost exclusively on the figure of Jack, it portrayed him as a romantic, a gentleman adventurer and a throwback to the great days of British imperial exploration. The *Edmonton Journal* set the tone, calling Jack an 'eminent explorer' with a 'love of the wild' who was 'regarded as knowing more about that country than anyone in the north'. In London, *The Times* said he 'had a roving and adventurous temperament', and gave a grossly exaggerated assessment of his importance:

> On account of his extensive knowledge of Northern Canada he was offered an important post in the Canadian government, but did not accept it. He was one of the first white men to discover the white Eskimo and the Eskimos generally knew him as the 'little father'.

Meanwhile, the *South China Morning Post* likened him to Lawrence of Arabia.

There is no surviving evidence of how Edgar's parents viewed the letters and reports which treated the Thelon deaths as noble repetitions of Scott. But some close to the family seem to have had doubts about it. One of the colonel's aunts, eighty-five-year-old Violet, wrote of her sense of unnecessary waste: 'I know he went out with such spirit, such great hopes.' And from an old employee, Mildred Greenwood, came this:

> I have just seen the Paper & feel sure it must be the 'Little Edgar' I taught his letters to at Earl's Barton grown to a man. It is terribly hard to lose them, dear, when you have watched them grow up, but there must be some hidden purpose we cannot see.

A year later, the public view was to swing to some extent behind these more humane responses. In 1930, the *Daily Mail* printed extracts from Edgar's diary, provoking a new sackful of mail for Bron Dirion. But now expressions of regret and loss outweighed the imperial heroizing. For every correspondent holding the view that 'Your son's name has been added to the role of British heroes', there were several who saw a tragedy rather than a disguised triumph. In this perspective, as the innocence and pathos of Edgar displaced the prowess of Jack, the deaths seemed no longer stirring but pitiful and close to hand.

I trust God will comfort you and make clear the whys and wherefore of that child's privation and suffering.

My heart aches for you all. I can understand a little of the agony of mind you must have been through.

I take the liberty of writing a few lines to you & Lieut. Colonel Christian to convey my sorrow at the loss your son Mr Edgar Vernon in the Arctic, being a *Daily Mail* reader. There was a graphic account & when I read his letter to you and brothers and sisters I felt sure it was the family I worked for at Plymouth, Woodland Terrace.

When Colonel Christian decided in 1937 to publish *Unflinching: A Diary of a Tragic Adventure*, with the text of the diary in full and extracts from the letters home, he did so explicitly 'in the hope that it may reach some of the rising generation and inspire them with courage, loyalty, and endurance'. This had some unexpected side-effects. In 1938, a German edition was published, after which Edgar's father received a letter from his publishers informing him that 'The German youth organization HITLER-YOUTH is very interested in *Unflinching*' and was asking permission to reproduce some of the book's photographs in their official paper 'as an example of fortitude and of all what is valuable in men'. But the book's publication also tended to expose the full pity and waste of Edgar's death. This was not always appreciated at the time, even outside the ranks of the Hitler Youth, yet not only did it reveal the author as pathetically trusting, it unwittingly raised compelling doubts about Jack on almost every page.

No one, indeed, is likely to close the book today without wondering about Jack Hornby, and what he thought he was doing attempting to live without supplies and with two greenhorns in one of the most hostile spots on the planet. It is clear from its pages that the party had difficulty feeding itself from the very first. And, while it might take a specialist to pick up the ineptness of their fishing, or their attempts to net ptarmigan, it must be clear to all that they carried too little dry food, deficient clothing and inadequate ordnance.

Those who knew both Jack and the North, while allowing that they had been moved by *Unflinching*, were particularly caustic about the book. A copy exists in which the annotations of Douglas, Critchell-Bullock and O.S. Finnie are collated. Against Edgar's judgements that 'anybody who is with J. Hornby can never go wrong' and 'Jack has very sound ideas', George Douglas scrawls in the margin of his copy 'Poor kid'. Where Edgar writes 'most men take supplies', Douglas comments 'Too bad *they* didn't!' and beside the sentence 'he has the reputation of living off the land only, without any white man's grub', the note is 'Off Indians and Trappers!'

These views were recorded at O.S. Finnie's request, who collated them in his archive with those of Guy Blanchet, Vilhjalmur Stefansson and others who knew Jack Hornby well. Finnie's own reflections are particularly damning of Jack's part in the debacle. Where the editor of *Unflinching*, Drew Roberts, advances a Scott-like justification that:

Hornby had been defeated by the incalculable factor which upsets all reckoning between men and the forces of nature. Here it had been some mysterious change in the normal migration of the caribou [and] a winter exceptionally long even for those regions.

Finnie writes:

These factors are not incalculable and should be taken care of as they usually are in the North by common sense and intelligence. 'Poor Richard' says truly: 'Where sense is lacking, *everything* is lacking.'

Guy Blanchet sent his own comments on the published diary to George Douglas. He probed more deeply into Jack's lack of common sense, and was less inclined than Finnie to call it culpable.

Probably at best his [Hornby's] life was a fantastic form of escape. I doubt if he ever found much satisfaction or contentment, but his mind did not drive him. I don't think either yesterday or tomorrow mattered much, and today was controlled by whims. I think he was a chap who could lose himself in any small thing of the moment.

Douglas, like Blanchet, tended to exonerate Jack on grounds of diminished responsibility, shifting the blame for the disaster on to Edgar's family. Had they requested it, several friends and relations in Canada, such as Cecil Armitstead, could have enlightened them about Jack's credentials as a leader of expeditions. The Christians, apparently, did not contact them and were left with the 'English' view of their cousin – a fatal view since, in Douglas's words, 'England is the last place to look for truth about Hornby's capabilities.' In 1950, Douglas wrote to Blanchet:

> I hold Edgar's parents much to blame for letting their boy go off with a man of whom they knew nothing except his own glamorous version of himself.

And on another occasion, Douglas considered that Jack

> was certainly carried away by a 'Fantasy of his own imagined excellence' – and, most unfortunately, so were the parents of Edgar Christian.

As far as it goes, all this is true of Edgar's parents. But as an explanation for the deaths of Jack, Harold and Edgar it is too partial and reductive. Colonel Christian may indeed have made enquiries in Edmonton or Onoway. But there were many around there who had always believed in Jack Hornby.

A myth, once established, is hard to break down, particularly when it confirms the wishful thinking of an entire class. Jack's irrationality, which appeared with such clarity to the professionals who had known him in the North, and which is even more apparent today, was perfectly opaque to anyone predisposed to his heroism. Such people simply accepted Jack's reputation, even though it was to some extent the result of self-promotion, as a man with no interest in money or creature comforts, a man who stripped the core values of his class – chivalry, honour, endurance and courage – down to their essentials. There was a kind of perfection in his mode of life. It showed those values shining out, clear of contradictions and compromises, against a background of perfect and sublime desolation. It was in order to bear witness to the same values that Colonel Christian published *Unflinching*.

Dover College in due course added their ex-pupil, in other ways so undistinguished, to their roll of honour. The school chapel has a commemorative plaque to Edgar, dedicated on 13 May 1934. Meanwhile, the original diary is enshrined in the headmaster's study – a relic, cased under glass for public veneration. A sonnet by the Reverend James W. Mills was composed to commemorate the diary's arrival at the school. Mills's lines, which originally hung in a frame on the wall above the diary, are a blend of imperialism, pedagoguery and Muscular Christianity – the very stuff from which Jack's expedition itself had been formed. As poetry they are lame. But as an elegy for Edgar's young soul, they seem quite appropriate:

> *More than a diary lies here – content*
> *And core of English boyhood. You who read*
> *This tale of high emprise, this simple creed*
> *Of uttermost faith, this splendid argument*
> *In furtherance of our school, will soon be sent*
> *On your sole destiny. Your charactered seed,*
> *Before it burgeon amidst wealth or need,*
> *Awaits unknown particular event.*

O Christian! Proving title to thy name
Through wastes of dereliction stark and slow,
What shriving priest hadst thou? What guide to tend?
Unless indeed the Great Explorer came
And helped thee make — as He made long ago —
Last love-links with thy Mother and thy friend.

18. The Death of a Lancer

Many other men and women, all older and wiser than Edgar Christian, had tales to tell of Hornby and the fatal charm of his legend. But James Critchell-Bullock's story remains the most interesting, as well as the saddest. George Douglas once remarked that the encounter with Jack Hornby had had a 'catastrophic' effect on the captain. And, though it was not so immediately baleful as Edgar's own experience, 'catastrophic' is not too strong a word. The 1924–5 expedition had not only ruined Critchell-Bullock financially, it had shaken his belief in his own judgement. How could he, an officer of the Indian army who had served in Baluchistan, marched into Jerusalem with Allenby and fought on the Western Front, have been taken in by one so obviously irresponsible as Hornby?

During 1924, in the first flush of expedition fever and government sponsorship, Critchell-Bullock had accepted a fellowship of the Royal Geographical Society – virtually the ruling body of British imperial exploration. Then he had seemed on the brink of a dazzling new career as an explorer, even a future holder of the Society's ultimate accolade, the Gold Medal. Now all these hopes were in ruins and the memory of them would pursue him for the rest of his life.

Critchell-Bullock's written recollections of Hornby, of which there would be many, were usually tinged by hindsight and *hauteur* and tended to dwell obsessively on Hornby's faults. Yet, on hearing in 1928 of his former partner's death, he wrote to George Douglas in terms that are extraordinarily immediate as well as emotional:

> As you know, no finer trail companion for the man he liked ever lived, and his astonishingly fine character-istics have, during the past two and a half years, returned to my memory so vividly that I regard him, and shall continue to regard him, as the most lovable creature I ever knew.

This seems difficult to square with the earlier fierce resent-ment at Hornby's having ruined Critchell-Bullock's finances and his reputation. But the captain's feelings always swung between clear-eyed realism and the revived memory of his old hero-worship.

Not long after he saw Hornby at Ottowa in November 1925 – for the last time, as it would turn out – Critchell-Bullock was forced to accept that his partner would default on all financial obligations. Jack had expended next to nothing on their costly outfit, despite (at least, as the captain under-stood him) having said he would meet half the expedition's expenses. Critchell-Bullock had tried hard to get his money. He had sent no less than eleven successive cables to Hornby in England, asking for remittances of cash, but received no satisfaction. One of the cablegrams was intercepted by Ada Hornby at Nantwich and she was furious with her son for getting this far into debt. He told his mother that none of it was true and that he owed nothing.

It must be presumed that Critchell-Bullock, if he was prepared to put himself through this sickening humiliation, was genuinely facing destitution. For the moment he had the Canadian Government's grant of $600, in payment for his report, but this would soon be gone. Then he would be a 'gentleman' on his uppers, with no trade and severely limited prospects. In one entry in his diary, written on the trail towards the end of the journey, he had already faced this possibility with a kind of lugubrious relish.

> I see long lean years of trials ahead of me, and hardship in civilization is a thousand times worse than it is here. No one in civilization has any use for a penniless gentleman because, of course, he is a failure. And again. What earthly use is a gentleman anyway? My short experience of Canada was sufficient to show pretty conclusively that a bricklayer, professional bar-keep, or experienced clerk has a better chance of finding employment than any man whose 'advantages' consist of guts, education and a sort of Jack-of-all-Trades knowledge.

After finishing his report – a substantial 245-page document – he spent some time trying to persuade O. S. Finnie to back a new expedition, the investment to be repaid with profits from the sale of new wildlife movies. Finnie, who may first have requested a screening of Critchell-Bullock's existing footage, turned him down and the disappointed explorer left Ottawa in disgust. He made for New York where, from the Explorer's Club in West 76th Street, he set about trying to market the films he had shot with Hornby. He found that no one in the city would touch them.

By now, Critchell-Bullock was aware that Hornby was missing in the Barrens. He wrote again to the Canadian authorities, this time offering to lead a rescue party, but was again turned down. When finally he heard the news that all three men had been found dead beside the Thelon, he felt an odd sense of guilt.

> I was bowled over completely . . . I have felt that in a measure I was to blame. I ought to have been on that trip and, had I been, Hornby would never have left equipped as he was.

In the course of 1928, Critchell-Bullock made a coast-to-coast drive through America as the Depression began, giving lectures on the caribou and the musk-ox and showing his films in any small town that would hang up a sheet to make a screen. This itinerant life was attended by many problems and break-downs in out-of-the-way places. 'I ground my teeth and swore consistently all the time, but except for the misadventures the trip would have meant little to me.' Meanwhile, he fantasized about farming white fox in the Barrens.

Eventually the captain found himself in San Francisco, where he was reduced to a position with the Press Syndicate of New York, 'publishers of expensive editions which are sold by direct sales methods'. Although describing himself as 'General Manager of the interests of the firm in the west', Critchell-Bullock was a door-to-door encyclopaedia salesman, working on commission. He smarted painfully at the indignity.

All this time he did not – could not – forget Hornby. He had written 'several tens of thousands of words' in four unpublished articles on him, as well as a 75,000-word draft of a 'novel' about the preliminaries to their expedition, which was submitted to at least one publisher and rejected. In early 1929 he was interviewed by a young San Francisco journalist, Malcolm Waldron, who himself had ambitions to be an author, and the two concocted a new book on the expedition, with a text by Waldron, 're-written rather than written from the amazingly extensive diaries and records of Captain James C. Critchell-Bullock'. Although Waldron was suffering from pulmonary tuberculosis, and would die before the book was printed, he completed the work in time for it to be accepted by the publisher. It appeared in 1931 under the title *Snow Man: John Hornby in the Barren Lands*, and was a modest success, with Critchell-Bullock enthusiastically throwing himself into the publicity. Yet he was later to denigrate Waldron's 'sensationalized account', which was, he said, interested only in his and Hornby's 'grotesque hardships' on the trail.

Waldron had somehow got it wrong and Critchell-Bullock worried anew about how best he could express what Hornby had meant to him. But further financial problems intervened. In 1930, after accumulating some savings, he was 'case-skinned' in California by a 'scoundrel' who cheated him of his money over the purchase of a boat. He had hoped to sail her north, around Alaska and up the Mackenzie River. But with that scheme now in ruins, he moved on to Vancouver, where he dreamed up a trip to prospect for gold at the headwaters of the Liard River. After a few months, the firm that employed him went bankrupt, and Critchell-Bullock despaired of his prospects in North America. In 1932 he returned, for the first time in a decade, to England.

Two years later, Critchell-Bullock resigned from the Royal Geographical Society. It must have seemed like a final acceptance of his fate, which was not, as he had ardently hoped, that of a successful explorer but of a dull, desk-bound businessman. Paradoxically, the more he affected to despise England and office work, the more he prospered. Soon he held a clutch of directorships and had sufficient means to live comfortably in Eaton Place, at the smart centre of London's Belgravia. After the Second World War, during which he had helped organize and run a unit of the Home Guard, he claimed to draw an enormous net income of £10,000 a year from 'seven directorships'. He also had a wealthy new wife, 'half my age'.

But in the late forties England had a Labour government, which Critchell-Bullock detested, and was still in the throes of a stultifying postwar austerity. The birth of a son 'cinched it' for him. 'I could not see myself trying to make a man out of a lad in an over-ripe kind of civilization.' He decided to sell up at a considerable loss and take his family to Kenya. In this action an old pattern was repeating itself: Critchell-Bullock, in search of 'fresher country', would eventually make himself penniless, just as he had in 1925. The difference was that this time he would also lose his life.

The Critchell-Bullocks had arrived in Nairobi in May 1950, in a mood of bullish optimism and with £25,000 in capital and 'four tons of antique furniture and effects'. He liked the country and its people 'barring some of the hoodlums exported by the Socialist government for State-aided projects'. The pioneering spirit was alive in him, but so was something which looked very like Jack Hornby's old carelessness about the future. Critchell-Bullock had no fixed plans for what he would do in the colony. Surveying the scene from the comfort of his first address, Nairobi's Norfolk Hotel, he vaguely considered opening a drive-in cinema because, as he thought, 'if I can introduce a few creditable (and, we'll hope, profitable) undertakings to the country, I shall get the hang of the land and learn what to do next'. For a man of the captain's military instincts, this looks dangerously unmethodical.

He had not been in Kenya a month when he felt the stirrings of an old obsession. A letter reached him from Vilhjalmur Stefansson in New York, requesting a biography of their mutual friend Jack Hornby for the projected *Encyclopaedia Arctica*. To a man who had once sold encyclopaedias, there was considerable satisfaction in being asked to write for one, and Critchell-Bullock set to work immediately. Stefansson (and Douglas when he saw it) thought the result – a seven-page, single-spaced typescript – brilliant but not entirely objective. In the end, the encyclopaedia project did not flourish and Critchell-Bullock's effort was never published.

The essay is a distillation of all his feelings about his former partner, in places waspish and debunking, in others almost elegiac. This unevenness suits Hornby's character and, despite its subjectivity, the piece amounts to a persuasive portrait of a highly contradictory figure. Hornby's physical courage, or indifference to danger, is not doubted; indeed it is praised. He could be a man of the highest standards of honour and principle, yet at the same time was a 'stunt-merchant', a futile explorer and a boaster, with the dirtiest personal habits on the trail and a debilitating hatred of modern equipment. If 'not the traveller that he thought he was', he could nevertheless be a 'captivating, charming man'.

Plunged back into the past, re-reading *Unflinching* and *Snow Man*, Critchell-Bullock brooded on the disaster that had overtaken Hornby, Harold Adlard and Edgar Christian on the Thelon. He had never been, in truth, very much affected by the fates of Edgar and Harold. He always considered that, dulled as they were by privation, they hardly suffered. But he had tried hard over the years to empathize with Hornby's agony. Years ago, when *Unflinching* appeared, he had written to Colonel Christian a rather discomforting letter of appreciation.

> I have often felt my flesh creep at the thought of what he [Jack] must have suffered mentally when he had to face up to the inevitable. The pride of the man was so immense, and his affection for your son was, from what friends who met them both have told me, so real that the whole show must have been torture.

A certain amnesia towards his partner's behaviour on the Casba River at Christmas 1924 is evident in this sentiment. Could a man like Jack Hornby, so egotistical and confident of his own superiority, have really suffered mental anguish before he died? By the time he wrote his 1950 essay, Critchell-Bullock no longer cared to speculate on the question. He merely observes that Hornby 'gambled, and he lost'.

In Kenya, Critchell-Bullock too had gambled. He sank all his money in an up-country asbestos mine, sending samples to George Douglas in Ontario for analysis. But it was the time of the Mau-Mau uprising and, whether for this reason or some other, the mine was slow in turning a profit. With his money bleeding away, Critchell-Bullock was slowly being reduced once again to a 'penniless gentleman'. His father-in-law, furious at the threat to his daughter's patrimony, travelled to Nairobi and confronted the captain in private. What form the discussion took is not recorded, but it appears that Critchell-Bullock was handed a loaded revolver before his father-in-law left.

On 30 March 1953, the captain took the required action. He did not consider, in his mid-fifties, that he could start again. He did not think he could bear penury, or its alternative, a return to the 'overblown civilization' of England. So he made his way alone to his former address, the luxurious Norfolk Hotel, and took a room in the single-storey residents' wing. Through the night he wrote letters, including a brief one to the secretary of his club, resigning his membership, and another to the hotel manager, Abraham Block, whom Critchell-Bullock knew quite well. This read:

> Please pardon me for doing you such a thoroughly bad turn! I should have preferred to kill myself elsewhere but with the Mau-Mau rampant, I had to consider the confounded revolver.

261

I hope the enclosed cash will at any rate settle my bill! Incidentally I am not getting out of the way because my mining venture was unsuccessful. On the contrary it augurs extremely well for the colony. And neither am I in debt. It is just one of those old, old stories: relations-in-law.

All the best to you and do not let this upset you more than you can help, old chap.

Laying down his pen, Critchell-Bullock spread several thicknesses of newspaper across the bed. He bathed, and dressed in crisp new pyjamas and a dressing-gown. Then he lay down and carefully shot himself. It was five a.m. The guest in the next room thought the sound was a backfiring car and went back to sleep.

The captain's body was found next morning by the chambermaid, sprawled amongst blood-soaked newspapers. A neat stack of suicide notes lay on the writing desk nearby.

A Note on Sources

The original of Edgar Christian's diary is preserved at Dover College while the text has been published in two editions under different titles. *Unflinching* (London, 1937) was edited by B. Drew Roberts, while a more scholarly edition by George Whalley appeared as *Death in the Barren Ground* (Ottawa, 1980). This has, in an appendix, the police report on the finds in the cabin, dated 1929. All non-diary quotations from Edgar's writings are from three letters to his parents, written during the trip and dated 7 May, 7 June and 10 June 1926. Colonel Christian's farewell letters to Edgar are dated 12 and 26 April. A few details of life at Dover College in 1924–5 have been gleaned from *The Dovorian*, and letters of condolence on Edgar's death are courtesy of Hazel Lunt.

On Hornby, Whalley's full-length study *The Legend of John Hornby* (London, 1962) is essential reading. *Snow Man: John Hornby in the Barren Land* by Malcolm Waldron, which was first published in 1931, is interesting both about Hornby and Critchell-Bullock, though heavily romanticized. A new US edition, introduced by Lawrence Millman, appeared in 1997. Waldron valuably quotes a few passages from Hornby's lost diary of 1920–22, while Hornby's Caribou Report of 1925 appeared as 'Wildlife in the Thelon River Area' in *Canadian Field Naturalist* 1934 48 [7] and is reprinted in Whalley, 1962 (as Appendix A). An account of the young

Hornby is in George Douglas's *Lands Forlorn* (New York, 1914), and a number of autographed letters from Hornby are preserved among Douglas's papers in the Canadian National Archive, Ottawa. This also holds further correspondence about Hornby between Douglas, Blanchet, Stefansson, Critchell-Bullock, Finnie and others and has been exhaustively consulted.

The prime source for chapters one and eighteen, and for much in between, is the writings of James Critchell-Bullock. The most important are his unpublished diary of the 1924–5 expedition, the typescript of his official report on the same, entitled 'An Expedition of Biological Research to Sub-Arctic Canada, 1924–5', and his later biographical sketch of Hornby, also unpublished, for the proposed *Encyclopaedia Arctica*. I have also made use of letters by Critchell-Bullock to Douglas, Stefansson and Colonel Christian and, in respect of the captain's last days, I have referred to Jan Hemsing, *Then and Now: Nairobi's Norfolk Hotel*.

Chapter two's account of Commander Evans on the Great Ice Barrier is drawn from his *South With Scott* (1921), while Francis Thompson's ten-line poem, written to commemorate a cricket match played in 1878, is entitled 'At Lords'. There is no published biography of Jack Hornby's father, but I am indebted to the researches of W. H. Hoole, privately printed under the title 'The Cricketing Squire'.

The only literary remains of Harold Adlard are a few passages from his letter to his parents, written from the Barren Lands on 12 August 1926. These are quoted in a story in the *Liverpool Post*, 3 October 1929. Two articles from 1978 with a bearing on the story are 'I found the bodies of the

Hornby party' by Kenneth M. Dewar and 'Soviet satellite debris hits historic area and recalls tragic Hornby drama of 1927' by Robert Common (both *Canadian Geographic* 97 [1]). C. H. D. Clarke's unpublished talk to the Arctic Explorers' Symposium, Toronto, 1978, is also useful, as is 'Observations and Explorations Along the Thelon River' – a report of the Thelon Heritage River Expedition 5–29 July 1991 (Canadian Parks Service).

Of general books consulted on the North, I would mention R. M. Ballantyne, *Hudson Bay* (1850), Vilhjalmur Stefansson, *My Life With the Eskimo* (1913), Lewis R. Freeman, *The Nearing North* (1928), Helge Ingstadt, *Land of Feast and Famine* (1933), Erik Munsterhjelm, *The Wind and the Caribou* (1953), and Pierre Berton, *The Mysterious North* (1956). Of more historical interest are volumes by J. W. Tyrrell, D. T. Hanbury and George Back. David F. Pelly's relatively recent *Thelon: A River Sanctuary* (Merrickville, Ontario, 1996) contains an excellent bibliography.

For the general cultural background, four works have been particularly illuminating: *Farewell the Trumpets: An Imperial Retreat* by James Morris (1978), *The Return to Camelot: Chivalry and the English Gentleman* by Mark Girouard (1981), *The Arctic Grail: the Quest for the North-West Passage and the Pole 1818–1909* by Pierre Berton (1988) and *I May Be Some Time: Ice and the English Imagination* by Francis Spufford (1997).

N

S

To MacDonald

McKINLEY'S PORTAGE TO

CANOE PORTAGE TO MACKAY LAKE

HOUSES

BOULKER'S NARROWS

HANBURY CREEK

DARK

HANBURY'S PT

HOUSES

HOUSE

BOU...

...CHANNEL

S T A R K ' S IS.

MACTONALD R.

McDONALD

McSWAIN IS.

McKINLEY'S PT

WOODMAN IS.

C H R I S T...
BAY

KEITH PT

ROX I.

BLANCHE I.

BARGUIST

PLANCHET'S CHANNEL

WILSON'S ISL.

KINGS CHANNEL

SOUSIE KINGS

ISLAND

MERCREDI IS.

HORNBY'S CHANNEL

MERCREDI CHANNEL

WILSON MINE

ROS GOULAIS IS.

BY REPORT CANOE CHANNEL

RABBIT ISLAND

PEARSON'S BAY

MERCREDI PT

TALSON BAY

PEARSON'S NARROWS

HOUSES

REMAINS

OLD FORT

X HOUSES   X HOUSES

PICARRE LE LOCHE RIVER

TALSON R.

ON

Same, Game- ...
Caribou. Before the ...
come to the N.E. on ...
reader they of ...
in the winter 1919 ...
land caribou) can ...
as Talson River ...
leave before the ...
any bulls are to ...
up of the ice ...

Moose & black bear ...
to found anyw...
Red foxes are scarce ...
either are very scarce.
White Foxes is some...
very plentiful in w...
Wolves & Wolverine are...
plentiful in winter,
marten & mink scar...
Lake
other a few N.E. of ...
... scarce
...N.E. of Falcon...

L.S. Large Dwelling.
S.W. of ROY. I.
S. Small Dwellings
S. ACT. S
& sometime
M. Kinley TP.